Literacy in the Digital Age

Reading, Writing, Viewing, and Computing

Frank B. Withrow

SCARECROWEDUCATION

Lanham, Maryland • Toronto • Oxford
2004

Published in the United States of America
by ScarecrowEducation
An imprint of The Rowman & Littlefield Publishing Group, Inc.
4501 Forbes Boulevard, Suite 200, Lanham, Maryland 20706
www.scarecroweducation.com

PO Box 317
Oxford
OX2 9RU, UK

British Library Cataloguing in Publication Information Available

Library of Congress Cataloging-in-Publication Data

Withrow, Frank B.
   Literacy in the digital age : reading, writing, viewing, and computing /
Frank B. Withrow.
      p.   cm.
   Includes bibliographical references (p.   ) and index.
   ISBN 1-57886-033-4 (pbk. : alk. paper)
   1. Computers and literacy.   2. Education–Effects of technological
innovations on.   I. Title.
LC149.5 .W58 2004
302.2'244–dc21   2003014105

∞ ™ The paper used in this publication meets the minimum
requirements of American National Standard for Information
Sciences—Permanence of Paper for Printed Library Materials, ANSI/
NISO Z39.48-1992. Manufactured in the United States of America.

CONTENTS

PREFACE

Reading is the core subject in elementary school. Young children are eager to go to school because that is where reading is learned. Thanks to many television programs like *Sesame Street*, many children are prepared for this adventure in literacy. Many parents have spent time reading to their children daily. Many children have their own libraries of audio and videotapes as well as books. My nine-year-old granddaughter wants to be a librarian so she has organized her books, tapes, CDs, and DVDs in her room and has created library cards for her friends who might want to borrow from her. We are raising children in a world that is full of images, codes, graphics, and text. In many ways, this is the age of imagination and literacy.

Parents, teachers, grandparents, and others are interested in seeing each child learn to read. The digital world has placed the great library resources of the world at anyone's fingertips. In a simpler time, scholars and scribes controlled the stored information of society. Today, anyone can have access to a multiple array of information and knowledge. The have-nots, the illiterates, are the disadvantaged of this modern world. The quality of life for those who have not mastered digital literacy skills is substandard. In a globally competitive world, they are destined to never cross the digital divide. Modern literacy is more complicated at the beginning of the twenty-first century than ever before.

This book examines the issues in society today and how digital technology is molding learning and teaching. Digital technology allows us to focus on the learner's needs and provide the learning materials and human resources needed to meet educational goals.

INTRODUCTION

We live in an ocean of digital data.
Data when organized becomes information.
Information when acted upon becomes knowledge.
Knowledge over time may become wisdom.

—Frank B. Withrow

Rich man, poor man, beggar man, and/or thief—we all live in an age where text pops up everywhere. Even the poorest homes in the United States have television, with its accompanying images, sounds, and text on screen. The challenge is how to use these signs, codes, and symbols effectively. As a society, we need to apply these resources to learning, comprehension, and teaching in order to develop a more productive and enlightened citizenry.

The average six-year-old entering school has watched approximately 9,000 hours of television. In twelve years, a high school graduate will have spent 12,960 hours in a classroom if the student has a perfect attendance record. During that same time period, the young person will have watched more than 20,000 hours of television. Most young children have a library of videotapes (now DVDs), audiotapes, CDs, and computer programs. Cameras are so cheap that they are now in disposable formats. Even digital cameras are cheap enough that many young children have them. Video games and computers are available to most families. Very young children are sophisticated in the uses of video and computer games. I met a seven-year-old who had a game on the nations and capitals of Africa. He quizzed me about Africa and I lost.

My twin great-granddaughters just returned from Disney World.

Their father used a digital camera and took 210 pictures of the twins with everyone from Mickey Mouse to Goofy. They shared this digital album with me through Shutterfly on the Internet. I could select the pictures I wanted from the 210 digital pictures and Shutterfly would send me hard copies of the photos. The girls know how to operate the Shutterfly site and view their album. They give running audio commentary as you view the slideshow. The most amazing thing is that five-year-olds take the technology for granted and can operate it with sophistication. The old joke that "if you can't program your VCR or computer, get a ten-year-old to do it" has a ring of truth. Technology is second nature to our children.

James P. Coleman, twenty years ago, wrote in a report that schools are not a real-world environment.[1] They do not give the learner the experiences they need in the real world. Measurements by tests are not indicators of what the student has learned and are relevant neither to the student nor to society. Technology opens up new vicarious experiences that can take place both within the school and outside the classroom. Technology also can provide real-world experiences and allow people of different ages to interact on common problems.

Since 1988, the distance learning programs of the U.S. Department of Education have been providing exemplary learning experiences through satellites, broadcast television, and the Internet to approximately two million learners annually. The Star School's e-learning distance courses are varied and range from elementary school science and mathematics, advanced placement, and foreign language courses to college subjects.

The Star Schools program, begun in 1988, has funded $452,153,186 in distance learning resources. The program has served at least 15 million students with courses up to and including advanced placement curriculum. The federal share of the program has been approximately $30.00 per learner, making it an incredibly efficient program. It is one of the most cost-effective and efficient programs, giving learners in isolated rural and urban areas access to advanced placement courses in science, mathematics, and foreign languages that would not have been otherwise available.

There are thousands of small schools in the country that cannot attract qualified classroom-based teachers to offer such advanced courses. One of the first students of the Star Schools program was from a small border town on the Rio Grande River in Texas. His senior class had seven members. He was the only student interested in science, mathematics, and foreign languages so he took all these courses through distance learning programs. He was admitted as a freshman to the Massachusetts Institute of Technology. He was just the first of countless students whose lives have been enriched by the Star Schools program.

Distance learning expands the choice of subject matter for many students and makes available to them high-quality learning experiences. Choice is injected into the system from home schoolers to gifted students seeking alternatives to the offerings available from their local school.

Campbell and others define reading literacy as "the ability to understand and use those written language forms required by society and/or valued by the individual. Young readers can construct meaning from a variety of texts. They read to learn, to participate in communities of readers, and for enjoyment."[2]

According to Sweet and Snow,

We have made enormous progress over the last twenty-five years in understanding how to teach aspects of reading. We know about the role of phonological awareness in cracking the alphabetic code, the value of reading practice in producing fluency. The fruits of this progress will be lost unless we also attend to issues of comprehension. Comprehension is, after all, the point of reading.[3]

We must go beyond the book to digital tools and develop literacy skills that include critical analytical skills that enable citizens to use technology efficiently and ethically. Our moral actions must be directed toward peaceful and positive applications of technology to society. Our most urgent need is to create a citizenry capable of ethical applications of our technical skills and knowledge. It is not enough to achieve scientific excellence without an understanding of its ethical applications. Technology is not an end in itself; it must be directed toward a goal. It enables us to do something better than we can do without it. Each new technology brings with it positive and negative effects.

Can technology provide us with a new literacy that becomes the foundation of our schools? American schools are the foundation that has enabled us as a society to become the most powerful economic and scientific nation in the world. Our traditional schools were founded on a technology, that is, the printing press. The printing press enabled mankind to produce cheap books and libraries. It has been the access to these resources of stored knowledge that allows teachers to impart the experience and knowledge of the past to new generations. The United States has long struggled with the concept of universal education for all. It is this universal belief that *all* children can learn that has enabled the United States to become the dominant world power. Since the digital world has changed the way we store and retrieve information, we need to rethink teaching and learning.

Technology will change the way we organize and operate our schools. We are no longer constrained by books and on-site teachers. For more than a decade, we have dreamed that technology can provide learning at any place and any time. As Gene I. Maeroff describes, we are providing e-learning at all levels of education and learners of all ages are taking advantage of the new technologies.[4]

Information and communication sciences have changed forever how people access past experiences and knowledge. The challenge of the twenty-first century is how to bring all children into the digital age. It is unlikely that the world will create the classrooms needed or prepare the teachers to have unschooled children attend classes. Therefore, if we are to leave no child behind, we must invent new and effective technological solutions to learning and teaching.

Kofi Annan, secretary-general of the United Nations, in a 1999 foreword in a report on the state of the world's children said,

> Literacy is an essential human right, a force for social change—and the single most vital element in combating poverty, empowering

women, safeguarding children from exploitative and hazardous labour and sexual exploitation, promoting human rights and democracy, protecting the environment and controlling population growth. Literacy is a path toward international peace and security. . . . One hundred thirty million children in the developing world are denied this right . . . almost two thirds of them girls. Nearly 1 billion people are illiterate . . . the majority of them women.

The United States of America can, in partnership with other nations, lead the way to a better education around the world. If the United States of America designs a new model for learning and teaching based upon interactive Socratic learning, then we can export it to the world. The objective of this movement must be literacy in a digital age for every child in the world. This worldwide challenge requires that we reinvent learning and teaching. Technology is a major solution that can fill this gap. It is not the only solution and it does not eliminate the need for human resources. It does, however, mean that the mentor/teacher will require a different kind of preparation to be effective in a digital world. It may also require that learning take place anywhere and at any time. We must go where the learners are and provide the resources needed for them to learn. Technology allows learning to take place in the home, the field, the library, the community center, the workplace, and hundred of other places. As Maeroff wrote in *A Classroom of One*, "online learning will give us new opportunities for learning, but brick and mortar schools will remain the central focus of schooling." Nevertheless, online Socratic tutorials offer a new and exciting option for learners.

We think of tutorial learning as one of the most effective models for learning ever invented. However, to be successful, the tutor must have a wide range of knowledge and experience. As President Kennedy said to a room full of Nobel Prize winners, they were the most august and informed group of individuals to dine at the White House since Thomas Jefferson dined there alone. The success of the Socratic tutorial method has always depended upon the quality of the tutor. Thomas Jefferson was a wonderful tutor for those he came in contact with, but there are few who have his wide range of knowledge and understand how to impart it to others.

While we have few people as accomplished as Thomas Jefferson, the development of lessons through computer software can provide each learner with a personal, knowledge-filled tutor. Such design depends upon understanding human learning and the knowledge of content. Teams of learning designers have the potential for creating a new Socratic dialogue that blends the power of computing, content, and the Socratic tutor. In effect, the new learning resource can be more than the sum of individual parts. The computer can be patient and pace learning at the student's rate. It can be "Thomas Jefferson," a true renaissance scholar with a vast array of information and knowledge that can be brought to the learning experience.

The "log" is available any place and any time and geared to the pace of the learner. The learning paths can be broken into elements that meet the special needs of the learner. For example, a learner who is deaf may have all the materials presented in visual modes, and a learner who is blind may have print translated into speech and descriptive visuals. As voice recognition and voice translations systems become available, the student may ask for explanations in other languages. Content can be basic and upgraded as new information becomes available. Although text and keyboards will remain one way for learners to interface with computers, much of the learning will be through direct speech by the learner. The computer will interact with the student through speech, visual, and textual expressions.

The power of the computer is that it can provide both macro and micro examples in the learning experience. For example, in explaining the technology of a nuclear energy plant, the program can take you inside restricted areas and demonstrate the operation of the plant. If the learner does not understand a physics principle, the program can take the learner outside the plant and provide tutorial learning of basic principles of physics. The design of the program can be based on discovery and constructivist models that lead the learner to his or her own understanding of the materials to be learned.

Validation of learning can be built into the Socratic tutorials. The computer program can be designed—in fact, must be designed—so that successive steps in learning are based upon the learners' responses. A well-designed system will be one through which no two students will follow the exact same pathway through the learning experience. In other words, the designers must provide enough alternative pathways so that most learners will be able to find the support they need to master the content. Great software should be designed so that it meets the needs of a number of different cultures, languages, and abilities of learners.

Since this type of programming is not inexpensive, it should be designed for the world market. *Sesame Street*, while not a software package, provides a model for how materials can be developed for worldwide markets. *Sesame Street* is in 130 nations and more than twenty languages. Some of the nations use it in its English form whereas others are co-produced in the host nation. The co-produced programs are in the native language and the sets are culturally relevant to the host country. Some characters such as Bert and Ernie speak a number of different languages. The live characters are actors and actresses from the host nation. This type of development is cost efficient.

There is a need for organizations, such as the United Nations, UNESCO, and the World Bank, to foster the multinational development of high-quality, Socratic, tutorial-based learning computer modules. It is only with sufficient funding that the best of these learning resources can be developed. The most urgently needed content area is a worldwide literacy program. Literacy is the foundation of all future learning for individuals. Once literacy is mastered, self-instruction can take place. Ever since the Gutenberg press made books inexpensive, a single literate person can use that wonderful teaching machine, the book, to explore the knowledge of the world. Books and libraries have been the foundation of stored and retrieved knowledge and experience the world over. Today, with the Internet, there is an even broader world that can open to the literate person.

We live in an environment that can produce literacy at a young age. Preliteracy skills are everywhere—even three-year-olds recognize the Golden Arches and know it is a McDonald's where they can get a Happy Meal. Toys "R" Us is recognized as the cornucopia of games and toys. Children view children's television classics such as *Sesame Street* and *Mister Rogers' Neighborhood*. The complex world of television becomes a part of most children's lives and is an integral part of their knowledge base. Most young children are heavy users of television, watching from five to seven hours per day. Television is an especially complex form of symbolic or vicarious experience.

For most of the history of mankind, the primary symbol system has been speech and language in oral/aural formats. Even today, speech is the first and primary symbol system used in everyday discourse. As effective as speech is, its very nature means it is transitory. That is, the signals are time-bound envelopes. Five thousand years ago, written symbols began to appear. Two forms of such symbols were created. One was pictographic or iconic in form and the other phonetic. Both represented spoken symbols. The iconic symbols were based upon whole words or thoughts and the phonetic symbols were based upon letter representations of the sounds of speech.

Both systems have advantages. The iconic sign or symbol can express the message rapidly, but is limited in that there must be a sign or icon for every message. The phonetic system is efficient because it has theoretically a one-to-one relation between the sounds of speech and the written symbols of the language. It is theoretically possible to have an alphabet that has a letter for every sound in every language in the world. In 1888, the International Phonetic Alphabet (IPA) was first published for that purpose. The IPA has one letter for each sound within a given language. Unfortunately, the IPA has been used primarily for scholarly research.

Before the printing press was invented, scholars and scribes used their own idiosyncratic systems of phonetic writing. However, once the printing press was developed and we were able to print mass messages in books and newspapers, we fixated on the number of letters in the alphabet and retained spelling forms that did not conform to the phonetic rules of a given language. Consequently, we lost some of the advantages of a phonetic alphabet. English spelling is especially complex in that English adopts words from other languages and accepts the spelling but anglicizes the pronunciation.

There are approximately forty-four sounds in the English language, represented by the twenty-six letters of the Roman alphabet. The twenty-six letters are combined 196 ways to represent the forty-four sounds. Therefore, English spelling is only semiphonetic in nature.

Richard Lederer in *Crazy English* discusses the inconsistencies between spoken and printed words:

> In English orthography there is a considerable difference between the sounds of words and their spelling. This state of affairs is created by the inadequacy of the Roman alphabet to represent all the sounds of English; our cheerful willingness to borrow words and with them, the conventional sounds from other languages; and, finally, the gradual changes in the way we pronounce words, most of which have not been matched by repairs in spelling. The result is that about eighty percent of our words are not spelled phonetically. In effect, we have two languages, one spoken and one written.[5]

English has approximately one million words, whereas the French language by comparison has only about 200,000 words. English is the most-used language in the world. The English language accepts thousands of words from other languages and incorporates them into English text. This book will examine the way children learn and how speech, language, text, and all symbolic representations of the real world influence learning, including television, computers, and the Internet.

NOTES

1. James Coleman was asked to study the needs of youth in 1984 for the president's science advisor.

2. J. R. Campbell, D. L. Kelly, I. V. S. Mullis, M. O. Martin, and M. Stainsbury, *Framework and Specifications for PIRLS Assessment 2001* (Chestnut Hill, Mass.: Boston College, 2001).

3. Anne Poselli Sweet and Catherine E. Snow, eds., *Rethinking Reading Comprehension* (New York: Guilford Press, 2003).

4. Gene I. Maeroff, *A Classroom of One: How Online Learning Is Changing Schools and Colleges* (New York: Palgrave Macmillan, 2003).

5. Richard Lederer, *Crazy English* (New York: Pocket Books, 1989).

ONE

How Do Infants and Children Learn?

Experience is outside and inside, and the skills that are required to know it are as diverse as experience itself: language, logic, the use of tools to scan the skies, the earth the eye.

—Madeleine Grumet

How does an infant begin to organize the world? How does learning take place? What happens if the infant is deaf, blind, deaf-blind, or otherwise disabled? How does that infant organize the thought processes? Language development is critical to child growth and development. Speech and language are the most common ways we code our private sensory experiences into public expressions. There are many speculations about how speech and language developed, but they almost certainly evolved from association with both external and internal sounds. Humans perhaps mimicked the sounds of the environment and animal sounds.

In simpler times, infants were closer to the daily activities of human life. The development of a communications system may have been much closer to the child's real-world experiences than it is today. Until a relatively short time ago in the timeline of human history, speech and language were the only code system used.

In the last twenty-five years, we have learned much about how the brain processes sensory stimuli and encode them into speech language and knowledge. The new technology tools available to researchers have enabled us to examine the brain as the person learns. The work of researchers such as Howard Gardner has enabled us to think of multiple intelligences.[1]

The computer allows us to chart the progress of learners' experiences as they master a skill or accumulate knowledge. Even in an area such as modern dance we have developed tools that can chart the physical movements of a dancer as the dancer begins to master the steps in a new dance. Through brain research, we now know that the infant learns nouns in a different area of the brain from verbs. As teachers begin to use technology and management and diagnostic tools, they should be better able to identify the areas that need more instruction in reaching the learner's goals.

Speech and language are the human's most important learning achievement. They separate humans from other animals and enable humans to live in social communities. Another giant leap for mankind was when mankind learned to transfer speech to print.

Written codes were developed some 5,000 years ago, but the printing press is less than 500 years old. It was only after the printing press was invented that we could think about universal literacy for all people. Prior to that time, the scholars and scribes controlled literacy. Once cheap books were readily available from the printing press, we invented what we now know as modern schools, that is, when we bring our young children together and impart information and knowledge through an intermediary known as a teacher.

Teachers gain their storehouse of knowledge and information through reading books and using libraries. In the not-too-distant past, the creators of knowledge were the same people who imparted that knowledge to others. However, as we became able to store knowledge, experienced teachers replaced the master scholars who had students sitting at their feet to gain wisdom. Learning was an apprentice process, whether it was pursuing a craft or intellectual knowledge. The Socratic dialogue with an all-knowing scholar sitting at one end of a log with the inquisitive student at the other end was the ideal model for learning. This tutorial system with the patient and all-knowing authority is expensive and difficult to operate.

For better or worse, the modern school system in the United

States has been remarkably effective and successful. It was and remains the stepping-stone for class mobility. It is the foundation for the climb up the ladder of social and economic success. It is the core of a democratic society based upon performance. It is the engine that has driven our industrial and technological successes. As photography and telecommunications evolved in the middle of the twentieth century, the primacy of the book began to change, and electronic codes and symbols began to emerge.

The question we must ask today is whether the traditional school should remain the major format for mass education. We are no longer confined to books and libraries as storehouses of information. Do we need a new model of education?

The fact that 130 million children around the world have neither a classroom nor a teacher emphasizes this worldwide emergency. This is true even though 161 nations signed an agreement in 1991 in Jomtiem, Thailand, to educate all children. These goals have been restated repeatedly by the United Nations and the World Bank. It is unlikely that we will build the classrooms and prepare the teachers that could bring education worldwide to every child. We are leaving countless children behind in the world and that is a formula for disaster.

> We are on the verge of a revolution, one enabled by computers and networking. The revolution, however, may stall before it starts due to lack of innovation. Effective technologies require careful development and long-term support and funding; it is not clear where these funds will come from.
>
> —Bob Tinker

Before the average child enters the first grade in the United States of America, she will have viewed 6,000 hours of television, listened to recorded stories, talked on the telephone, and perhaps used a computer and video game. The family and parents are the child's first teachers. Hart and Risley in their studies of early interactions among adults and children under two years of age have found that it is important to establish a dialogue between the child and the adult.

The number of verbal encounters between the infant and the adult has implications for the child's future verbal ability. When there is a large amount of interaction between the child and the adult, the child seems to learn words faster and develop a significantly larger vocabulary. This difference seems to remain even as the child grows. The researchers followed the original children in their studies until they were ten years old. Not only does the difference remain between the verbal and taciturn families' children, but also the highly verbal families' children increase their vocabularies at a faster rate than the taciturn families' children do. The long-term results indicate that difference appears as early as children two years old.

A GUIDE FOR PARENTS ON HELPING YOUR CHILD BECOME LITERATE

Research and common wisdom tell us that the family that reads to their young child will significantly increase the possibility of the child becoming a good reader. In a digital world, many signs, codes, and stimuli compete for the attention of the child. Therefore, we must understand that literacy in a digital age means the child must become competent in the use of a wide range of materials.

Perhaps the most crucial aspect of literacy is the ability to analyze and think logically about the information source. What were the objectives of the creators of the materials? How valid are the creator's assumptions? How do the stimuli relate to the real world? In the world of animated cartoons, Wile E. Coyote can fall off cliffs and get back in the chase. What about the validity of computer games and how do they relate to the real world of physics? How can you validate what is in the newspaper, on television, in books? These are questions that are important in the early years as well as when the child is older.

Parents need to not only read with their young children but also to talk with and question the child as they read together. In developing critical viewing skills with children, parents need to view programs with their children and talk about what they see. Children need not only to develop the mechanics of the skills of reading but also to develop critical thinking skills that allow them to question what they read and see. One area that is critical in television viewing is to help the child understand advertisements that are directed toward them. Is the toy really as big as it seems in the ad? Will it do the things the ad claims? How will it stand up under hard play? These are things that help the child develop critical analytic skills.

As the parents read with their child, the child learns that the spoken word has a written counterpart. This phonemic awareness is the starting point in developing literacy skills. Children like to have the same story read over and over to them. They learn the story and can "read" the book themselves from the pictures. Many children's stories have repetitive events. In the classic *Three Little Pigs*, the big bad wolf at little pigs' house says he will huff and puff and blow the house in. When reading with your child, let him begin to finish the sentence such as the big bad wolf said, "I'll huff and puff and blow your house in." Often books have such repeated phrases printed in a different color. You can encourage the child to point to these words when they say them. He will begin to associate the print with the spoken word.

Parents can play rhyming games with their young children. Sound games that identify the sound that starts or ends a word are also fun for the family. Older siblings can work with the young child as well as the parent. When the family is taking a trip, a simple game is for the children to observe things they see that start with a certain sound or to point out signs with certain letters. Rhyming games that increase vocabulary are also fun for the whole family. Lazy Daisy is such a game. The parent or child asks what is a goof-off flower? The answer must rhyme; therefore, a goof-off flower is a LAZY DAISY. What is an obese feline? That would be a FAT CAT. What is the chief of police? A TOP COP and so on. As the child gets older, this game can become more complex in that the rhymes must become multiple syllables.

My five-year-old twin great-granddaughters live several hundred miles from me and I do not see them as often as I would like. Therefore, I send them e-mail and write them stories that their par-

ents read to them. The following is an exchange I had with respect
to a couple of silly poems by e-mail. This stimulated the family to
have the girls write their own poems.

JOE'S TOE

I once had a friend named Joe.
He did not have a big toe.
He worried that he only had a little toe.
This disaster must have come from his foe.
It is so sad not to have a big toe.
It made him feel so low.
That's the sad tale of my friend Joe.

He was so sad he didn't want to play with me no moe.
I thought about what could make him go.
From a cabbage I made him a big toe.
That cabbage toe
On his foot I did sew.
Now my friend Joe
Can run both fast and slow.
That's what I did for my friend Joe.

Now my friend Joe
Has a smile on his face that makes him glow.
All because of that cabbage toe.
He can run both fast and slow.
I'm glad I helped my friend Joe.
He loves to wiggle that big toe.
Now it's time for me to go.
Goodbye Joe.
Joe has a lot of trouble with his toe.

JOE'S TOE ANOTHER TIME

As Joe walked down the trail
A great big gale
came across the bay
and blew open the gate.
The gate hit Joe's big toe.

They put Joe in a boat
And rowed him across the bay.
What did the doctor say?
Joe's toe is broke.
The doctor tied a bow
On Joe's big toe.
Joe, go home and rest your toe
On a nice soft pillow.
That's what the doctor said don't you know.

—Great Grandpa Frank

Thanks for sending us these poems. Skyla and Haley [five-year-old twins] really enjoyed them. They are now trying to think up some silly poems of their own!

Here's what they've come up with so far:
Sew toe
On friend Mo
Friend Mo going down the land
His toe lands on sand
Sew toe
On Po
He's walking down the lane
His toe lands on somebody's head
It's a humongous toe
Is he dead?
Then he got back his toe
And then his toe falls off again
On the humongous beach
But Mo and Po do not have the same toe
Po had the biggest toe

ANOTHER POEM:

Mo is Po's buddy
Po is a Teletubby
Po is friends with Mo
Po has the biggest toe
In the whole world

Then his toe growed and growed
But Mo didn't know
Then Po's toe looked like the whole world
Mo painted it green and blue
What did he know?

Thanks for inspiring the girls! We had lots of fun! These are their first real poems and I was surprised how easily rhyming and story-telling came to them.

—Love, Nikki

There are also memory games that families can play, such as con-centration and twenty questions that increase the child's memory and logical thinking. All families are limited in time these days, so the parents should plan special times when they can interact with their children. Obviously, for generations, the bedtime story has been a traditional time for reading with your child. Television viewing, however, is often used as a baby-sitter rather than a fam-ily event. Parents should monitor their children's television view-ing. It is important that the parents know what their young child is viewing and that they create times when they view with their child.

It is important to talk with your child about the television pro-grams and explain things that might be confusing to them. Can the cartoon character really fall off the cliff, be banged on the head, and get up and run around again? In advertisements for toys, can the toy really do what the ad says it can?

You should know what television programs and video games are teaching. What is the secondary message? There was a very popu-lar nature film named *Willie the Skunk* that had very strong second-ary messages. Willie was the only boy skunk and he was in con-stant trouble exploring the world. It was supposed to be a film about skunks, habitats, and nature. In reality, it had a very sexist theme and rewarded conformity and strongly punished curiosity. Girls were good and minded their own business. Willie's sisters were very proper skunks and always did what their mother wanted them to do. They followed the mother skunk in a straight line and apparently had no curiosity at all. Boys were bad and got into all kinds of trouble.

Video games are sometimes more difficult to do as a joint venture because children often have greater skill than their parents at such games. Nonetheless, it is important for the parent to become involved with the child in the use of these resources. Computer games and activities, especially on the Internet, can become very complex. For the older child, there are sites that are designed not to educate but to promote propaganda. There are thousands of hate sites; parents must work with their children to help them resist such propaganda and to evaluate the validity of Internet site claims. There are blocking software packages, but a determined student can find a way around them. Ultimately, the user must learn to analyze information and determine its truth. There is no substitute for the parent's guidance in these matters.

As the child grows older and begins to understand the coding system between speech and print, the family can read stories aloud, perhaps after dinner. A great family activity is to act out a book, especially at Christmastime or other holidays. As my grandchildren grew, we had a family tradition of the older grandchildren writing out the Christmas story or a favorite story such as "Frosty the Snowman" and then producing a grand play that we videotaped. The kids all read their scripts in these plays. Usually one of the fathers was the narrator, but each child no matter how small had a speaking/reading part.

My grandchildren who created these memories are in college now and they like to bring out the old tapes at Christmastime to show the younger grandchildren and great-grandchildren. These kinds of activities blend the multiple media that are a part of our information society. Inexpensive computer-generated videos today can create quite good media shows and duplicate them on DVDs. These are the scrapbooks of the digital world.

It is crucial that parents (and, in fact, the whole family) learn to read and write together. One of the responsibilities of parents is to develop curiosity in their children and to help them observe the world. It is first through the parent that the child begins to understand the world. I once had dinner in a restaurant that overlooked a river and a historic bridge. There were barges on the river and trucks and automobiles crossing the bridge. It was snowing and a rather bad night, and my friend and I were the only two people in the restaurant when a man and his eight- or nine-year-old son came in. My friend and I sat near the window where we could observe the barges on the river. We decided that this was the time that the father and son had as "quality time."

Unfortunately, other than a very few words, the father and son chose to sit far back from the riverfront windows. Other than a brief conversation about the food, they had almost no conversation at all. My friend and I, without eavesdropping, could not help but be astounded at the missed opportunities of this pair. I cite this example to show that even routine things are fertile with language opportunities that give the child several things. They can (1) build the child's observation abilities, (2) increase awareness and curiosity, and (3) expand vocabulary and language skills. These all help develop literacy skills in a digital age.

My five-year-old granddaughter was visiting us and my wife took her on Washington's Metro to the Smithsonian Space Museum. My wife talked with her about the Metro and pointed out the raised foot of pavement next to the track's edge and asked her what she thought it was for. Then she explained that the raised pavement enabled blind people to know where the edge of the platform was. Then when the blinking lights came on, they talked about that signaling for deaf people that the train was arriving.

Another woman was so astounded at this conversation that she asked my wife why she was explaining these things to a child who was so young. My wife explained that you can have complicated conversations with even young children and that they will learn. Later, I took this same granddaughter and a cousin on the Metro and sure enough, she explained in accurate details to her cousin that the rough edge of the platform helped blind people and that the blinking lights helped deaf people.

I once had a very smart four-year-old neighbor. I liked to talk with Suzy on the steps in the summer time. Once I obtained a very small Asian umbrella and gave it to Suzy. She examined it and then told me she would take good care of it. She went on to explain that it appeared to be very delicate and fragile and, therefore, she would have to protect it because it was a precious gift. Although Suzy was very intelligent, she did not just come up with this vocabulary from the blue. Her parents read to her and talked with her about things in the world. All parents can talk with and explain things to their children.

A friend of mine talks about how he watches television with his small grandchildren and questions them about how real what they see on television is.

Parents need to remember that they must keep an open line of communication with their children—even with the teenager who goes completely off into the deep beyond of tattoos, body piercing, and other things. Parents are entitled to set limits, but this does not always work. If in the young years parents have read and talked with their children about books and television, they will have created a foundation for open communications in later years.

It is important for parents to listen to what the children are telling them. Even very young children are eager to tell stories. Be sure to listen to what they are saying. There is the old joke that little Suzie asked her mother where she came from and her mother was prepared to give her a factual sex information education. Suzie listened and when her mother asked her if she had any more questions, Suzie replied, "Yes, Mary Jane said she came from Chicago and I just wondered where I came from?" Be sure you are on the same wavelength and talking at the child's level.

Once a child has learned to sound out and decode the written text, she will need to increase her vocabulary and to read with fluency. Richard Allington says that too many teenagers can read at the beginning level, but choose not to read.[2] People choose to read when they are fluent enough to gain information and enjoyment. To enjoy reading for entertainment purposes, one must be fluent enough that the story engages the reader without the distractions of the techniques of reading. If I am reading *Harry Potter*, I have to be fluent enough for the story to unfold in my mind's eye. I cannot be slowed down in my reading by struggling with the mechanics of the alphabet or I will not enjoy reading.

The advantage of a series of books like *Harry Potter* is that once the first book is read, the reader is familiar with the idiosyncratic characters and vocabulary of the books. It is like visiting old and familiar friends. On the other hand, if I am reading for information, I indeed read slower and more deliberately because I will be gaining new vocabulary that is technically relevant to the information. Again, parents and family can be helpful if there are discussions about what is being read.

Major news events such as the *Columbia* shuttle tragedy are carried on television, websites, magazines, and newspapers. The melding of all these news sources into an informed understanding of the event is a part of the digital world. Families that talk and share these resources are creating an effective literacy for the digital age. The 2004 presidential campaign has already started in the spring of 2003. A high school student studying the campaign can access speeches, websites, and an almost unlimited amount of information from the Internet.

Another personal example that may help families understand the digital world: My wife of fifty-one years died. The family, including the grandchildren, all prepared written materials for the memorial services. Each child read her best memory of her grandmother. Because Margaret had been in the Waves in World War II, she was interred in Arlington National Cemetery with a full twenty-one-gun Navy salute ceremony. My nine-year-old granddaughter attended the service and her father videotaped it.

Because they were from out of town, they went to the cemetery visitor's center and collected historical materials on the history of the cemetery, such as the Unknown Soldier's grave, the JFK memorial, and other relevant facts. They visited the Unknown Soldier's grave and the JFK eternal flame memorial and took pictures. When she returned home, my granddaughter had her mother help her prepare a PowerPoint presentation for her school class because she had missed school to come to the funeral service. She answered her classmates' questions, and the books and PowerPoint CD-ROM are now available in the school library. This experience and the sharing with her classmates make this even more realistic to her.

The many opportunities in today's digital world allow families and children to create their own multimedia scrapbooks. My five-year-old twin great-granddaughters have a DVD of Peter Pan. When I visited them a few months ago, they had prepared a song and dance for great-grandfather of "I'll Never Grow Old" from Peter Pan. The fireplace in their home has a platform and they used it as a stage. The performance was excellent, except that one of the twins in her excitement fell off the end of the stage. I asked them how they learned the song and dance and they proceeded to show me the song in the DVD. At five, they knew how to operate the equipment, slow it down, and replay what they wanted to see.

Our children are growing up in a technological age. I once bought a three-year-old a battery-operated toy. She immediately understood how to insert the batteries and begin to operate it. I was impressed at Christmastime with my preteen and teenaged granddaughters who used to play with dolls; now they have cars and houses for Barbie. They immediately understood the directions and began to assemble the toys.

Recent research with teenagers on what they think their teachers know about computers is interesting. Teenagers from rural and urban areas believe they have better computer skills than their teachers do. They believe teachers are not very good at understanding and using the Internet. The good news in this respect is that the new teachers who are replacing the old guard have grown up with technologies and are relatively sophisticated in their uses.

NOTES

1. Howard Gardner, *The Disciplined Mind: What All Students Should Understand* (New York: Simon & Schuster, 1999).

2. Allington, Richard L., *What Really Matters for Struggling Readers: Designing Research-Based Programs* (New York: Addison-Wesley Publishers, 2001).

Two

Signs, Codes, and Symbols

If we then ask about the nature and role . . . the reader's conception of what kind of story or text he is encountering or "reinventing"—we are in fact asking not only a morphological question about the actual text, but also a question about the interpretative processes that are loosened by the text in the readers' minds.

—Jerome Bruner

How do young children associate their sensory experiences into a meaningful public communication system?

How does an infant grow and develop an understanding of her world? This most marvelous of all human accomplishments takes place normally between birth and the first two years. The sights, sounds, smells, touch, tastes, and kinesthetic senses come together and result in a conscious awareness of the world in which the infant lives. In what form does the conscious image manifest itself in the mind of the infant? How does the infant organize the world environment in which she lives? How does the infant begin to express her wants? How do young children use their abilities to communicate to control the world in which they live?

When the infant is hungry, he cries until his needs are satisfied. The cry is a first level of expressive communications. The infant begins to anticipate the resolution of his wants when his lips touch the mother's nipple. The infant responds to signs within the environment. When the infant hears the mother approaching, he often begins sucking. As the mother approaches the baby, the mother begins making soothing sounds and saying that food is coming. Often the mere soothing sounds of the mother's voice begin the infant's feeding process, that is, he begins sucking in preparation for being fed.

During the first two years of life, there are thousands of small face-to-face dialogues between the caregiver and the infant. Hart and Risley have studied these interactions and found that there are major differences among families. Some families are very verbal and others are taciturn. However, regardless of the way the family communicates, the adult initiates interactions about 40 percent of the time and the infant initiates it 60 percent of the time. They further found a major difference in vocabulary was measurable at age two among children from different family groups.

A casual observation of the average two- and three-year-old does not differentiate between such children. Most children develop functional language that includes both receptive and expressive language skills. Speech is sufficient to get the child's wants fulfilled and the child understands much of the routine language of the home or nursery school. All normal children have a functional receptive and expressive language system.

Two groups of children do not develop this normal sequence of language: deaf children and deaf-blind children. Obviously, if hearing is absent or limited, the oral/auditory signals of speech and language are not associated with the sensory experiences of the infant. In the case of the deaf-blind infant, no visual correlate of the spoken word can become the natural linguistic symbol.

The young child's ability to associate and assemble language is amazing.[1] If the child encounters a live dog and the word *dog* is spoken, the child associates the word with the animal. After a number of encounters, the child associates the word *dog* with a generalized concept of all dogs and differentiates them from cats and other animals. Not only will he generalize the concept of dog to other real dogs, he will recognize pictures of dogs, and videos of dogs, plush toy dogs, and now even robotic dogs. When the child thinks of a dog, what form of imagery does it take in consciousness? In the beginning, does the infant have visual, auditory, tactile, and even olfactory senses associated with thinking of a dog? The infant rapidly understands that the shorthand of the spoken word *dog* can effectively be used. In short, the child has a little voice in his head that talks to him about his thoughts. A conscious stream of thought is an internal form of oral/aural symbols that dominates the images of our mind. As soon as a child has at least 1,000 words, that child becomes an efficient communicator in our modern society. The key to intellectual linguistic development is a significant increase in vocabulary.

What happens in a deaf infant who does not receive the oral/ aural expressive linguistic signals? Even with some residual hearing, the deaf infant will create a receptive communication system through her visual sense.

We need to understand the differences between receptive aural signals and visual signals. The sense of hearing is unusually efficient in a 360-degree global environment and does not require light. In fact, meaningful sounds can be deciphered from noise that is considerably louder than the spoken signal. Hearing is the primary warning system and can be alerted even during sleep and in the dark. Vision, on the other hand, requires minimum light sources and is directional. The receiver of visual signals must be looking at the expresser and there must be reasonable light. Hearing codes those sequences of meaningful sounds into transient envelopes of stimuli. The sound comes and goes. Vision, on the other hand, handles symbols spatially and can be studied over time.

The receptive communication systems of a deaf infant are optional. A child can learn American Sign Language (ASL), finger spelling, speech reading, or a combination of all three. The deaf child associates the signs with real-world experiences and begins an associative system that organizes real-world sensory experiences with the symbols of language. There are at most in ASL 3,000 signs as compared to 1,000,000 words in the unabridged English dictionary. Deaf people use finger spelling to expand beyond ASL and merge ASL with Standard English. The deaf person also uses many body language signals as well as the formal sign.

The Rochester Method was used for years at the Rochester School for the Deaf in New York. This method taught finger spelling as opposed to a combined or ASL system. Finger spelling in one sense is the writing of the English language in the air. As such, it is the only English system that might be called a pure phonetic system in that there is always a one-to-one relation between the finger sign and the letters used in words.

Finger spelling was originally developed by the Spanish as an aid in teaching speech to deaf children. Once deaf children versed in finger spelling associate the finger sign with the letter, they can recognize any word they know. If a deaf child's total expressive and receptive language is built around finger spelling, then the transfer to the printed text is a simple matter. Research has demonstrated that the average four-year-old can visually discriminate the letters of the alphabet.

NOTE

1. My wife and I had four children and adopted a deaf boy and an aphasic girl. We observed and carefully watched each child's speech and language development.

THREE

Multiple Literacies

Multimedia computers are the first technology that truly focus our multiple forms of intelligence—text-based, abstract, visual, musical, social, etc. As such, they can tap into and ignite the unique talents of each student.

—John Seely Brown

Reading and writing are no longer the single mode of literacy. Anyone who lives with teenagers has observed them studying while they listen to a CD, search the 'Net, and dial a friend on their cell phone. This ocean of information flows in, around, and through them while they snatch the bits of information they want to use from it.

I observed my adopted son from Ghana as he was preparing for his Ph.D. in microbiology. He was a determined young man and I thought his study habits persistent, but weird. He turned on the television, had a CD available, searched the Internet, and often called friends and spoke to them in a combination of English, French, and Ashanti. I thought this was utter chaos, but he sorted this out and has done exciting research work in microbiology. Now I understand it as normal.

In our modern world, our young people are bombarded with thousands of bits of information. Not only are they receiving this information, they are creating it. Many young people are talented in creating and expressing their ideas in multiple formats from text, audio recordings, video art forms, and music to mixed media through the computer.

Our challenge is how to teach children to be critical in both receptive and expressive communication modes. How do we verify and trust the sources of our information?

In a simpler time, we could rely upon the integrity of the news source. We knew the reputation of the newspapers and we could trust it. We knew that some papers had a liberal or conservative slant, but we expected them to be honest and truthful within those contexts. The recent scandal at the *New York Times* has given us second thoughts in these matters. Likewise, we understood that television news was less in-depth than the print media, but we could have some degree of understanding of the slants and biases of the television programs. Editorial boards review books while research journals have expert peer reviews that give us some level of confidence of the validity of the materials. Even here we have been disappointed in the system because it has not weeded out some research that is false.

For years we have known that nations and politicians use sound bites and direct propaganda. In some ways, this is the crucial element in our understanding that we need to teach crucial technology skills that enable the user to validate the information they have. In his 1946 Nuremberg trial, Hermann Goering testified

> Why of course the people don't want war. Why should some poor slob on a farm want to risk his life in a war when the best he can get out of it is to come back to his farm in one piece? Naturally, the common people don't want war. . . . But after all it is the leaders of the country who determine the policy, and it is always a simple matter to drag the people along, whether it is a democracy, or a fascist dictatorship, or a parliament, or a communist dictatorship. . . . Voice or no voice, the people can always be brought to the bidding of leaders. That is easy. All you have to do is tell them they are being attacked and denounce the pacifists for lack of patriotism and exposing the country to danger.[1]

Although Hermann Goering was not the first propagandist to understand how to use media to exploit his leader's goals, he was one of the first to understand the uses of media. He used a wide range of radio, parades, and print materials to get the message across.

With multiple literacies, the challenge is how to teach users to have confidence in the validity of the information they use. How do you organize the various streams of information that come to you daily? The Internet is especially difficult because it is a universal publication system. It is a system without editorial boards, peer reviews, or other safeguards that ensure valid information. The thousands of hate websites are examples of this propaganda machine.

The teenage daughter of a friend of mine was researching information on World War II. She searched for information about Hitler. She was referred to a neo-Nazi site, which began to send her unrequested information that the Holocaust was a conspiracy by Zionists and that no one died in concentration camps. She made the mistake of writing back that their information was wrong. She then began to be flooded with hate e-mails.[2] We need to regulate such sites and protect our children from such trash. On the other hand, we stand for freedom of speech. In the new world of multiple formats, this becomes a problem for our nation.

The worldwide consolidation of multimedia companies also poses a problem. When all of the news sources are the same and controlled by only a few companies, we have to worry about the validity of the news. How do we prepare young people to analyze the information they receive?

In a simpler time, we assigned information sources to different categories—that is, print, broadcast, and computer sources. Today, with multiple media sources, these all merge into a complex ocean of information. Some information in any of the formats may be peer reviewed and validated whereas other information may be little more than rumor. Because of the swarm of media professionals, we are often given overkill in the details of an event.

For example, in times of tragedy, we have reporters with microphones asking intimate questions of family members. In the recent NASA *Columbia* tragedy, we seemed more interested in getting reactions of family members of the crew than in information with respect to the cause of the disaster. While the team looking into the causes is doing a slow and deliberate scientific survey of the problem, their report will not be carried in the sensational details we found being reported about family members. Students must learn how to value such coverage.

How can we demand more accurate reporting? How can we ensure that editors are providing balanced and accurate reporting? What does the average citizen need to know about global warming, for example? We have two sides reporting opposite data. How can a user of information make a reasonable and logical decision?

Literacy in a digital age means that we are informed and logical decision makers. *Literacy* means that we comprehend and analyze the various multimedia sources and, in the context of our own life, make rational decisions. We must be ever vigilant and even skeptical with respect to the information we use.

NOTES

1. Hermann Goering's testimony at his Nuremberg trial.

2. A friend at a University of Maryland meeting on the use of Internet by students described her daughter's experience.

FOUR

Reading and Writing

Words exist because of meaning. Once you've gotten the meaning, you can forget the words. Where can I find a man who has forgotten words so I can talk with him?

—Chuang-tzu

John Henry Martin in his software program "Writing to Read" developed a program that emphasized the connections between writing and reading and believed that you could teach writing as a precursor to reading.[1]

Mildred A. McGinnis in her work with both children and adults with language disabilities developed the Association Method that matched writing and reading.[2] She associated phonemes with speech and used cursive writing and kinetic movements of cursive writing as a means of associating speech and language with text. Louisa Moats in her book *Speech to Print* details many of the elements that are in a report by the National Reading Panel.

Richard Allington and others are critical of the National Reading Panel report, saying that the report ignores much of the research on reading and reinforces programs that have been in place for the last thirty years. There has been an emphasis on phonetics for the last thirty years and tests show that third and fourth graders effectively decode and encode words.

The problem with young readers in the United States is comprehension. What happens in the fourth, fifth, and sixth grades is that we assume they can read because they can decode words. Unfortunately, the content significantly increases in these grades and learners must increase their understanding of the more advanced vocabulary and make logical conclusions as they read.

We might look to a natural control group, deaf children, to give us insight into the complexities of learning to read. As any teacher of deaf children can tell you, reading depends on the level of language development of the student. For example, Basic English has slightly more than 1,000 words, but is awkward to use. If you are limited to only a thousand words, then you must use them more often to get across your ideas. *Tom Sawyer* printed in Basic English would be a series of books several feet high.

The advantage of larger vocabularies is that the writer has many more refined ways to express ideas. For example, if you do not have the language of "disciple of Jesus Christ," you come up with "one of the twelve close friends of Jesus Christ who worked with him when he was alive." The bottom line is that the greater the person's vocabulary, the greater freedom he or she has in expressing experiences and ideas.

We have many areas of technical vocabulary that merge between the general public knowledge and expert knowledge. Technical language becomes common with frequent use. For example, television weather reporting has introduced the public to the technical vocabulary of meteorology. Consequently, cold fronts, warm fronts, highs and lows, and other similar terminology have all become a part of common language. The recent war in Iraq provided for the world a number of lessons on geography with maps and illustrations of that region of the world.

The early days of NASA space flights were filled with exciting television coverage that taught the general public some of the mathematics and science required to launch and recover space vehicles. The NASA Select television channel carries all space flights and monitors things from inside the space shuttle. Most cable companies carry NASA Select for public viewing. NASA and the U.S. Department of Education once sponsored a program entitled "Toys in Space." Children around the nation selected ten toys that would be used by the astronauts in free fall. The astronauts used the toys in free fall and then repeated the experiments in Earth's gravity. They explained the physics that were relevant in both space and on Earth.

Although children can learn many things through technologies, there are also some drawbacks. We have just so many hours in a day. If a young child spends six to nine hours per day watching television, searching the 'Net, or even practicing a sport, it will cut into the available time for reading and studying. Since the 1950s, television—for better or worse—has been an undefined curriculum for American children, and for that matter, children all over the world. It is a window on the world for children. It can be used for propaganda as well as for nonbiased educational purposes.

Children need to critically evaluate the advertisements that are directed toward them. Parents should monitor and talk with their children about the television they view. Although I have mentioned television, the issues are the same for the Internet, video and computer games, and other technologies. Children need to learn that these media are created by people and are therefore biased with respect to the creator's views. This, of course, is true for all forms of media, from books to the Internet.

The success of teaching reading and writing is dependent upon personal experiences and the language level of the learner. Hart and Risley have demonstrated the disparity among children as young as two years of age. Part of the challenge is how to reduce that difference and how to increase the rate of vocabulary growth among all children.

Language begets more language. Likewise, among good readers, reading begets reading. Language is not only associated with the sensory experiences of the learner; more sensitive and complex language comes from language building upon itself. Reading itself becomes a vicarious sensory experience for the reader, broadening actual experience. Concepts such as freedom, justice, liberty, and equality are not directly associated with sensory experiences, but are brought about through sophisticated uses and comprehension of language. Reading broadens the individual's experience base.

Reading and writing can be taught together. How should this be done? The National Reading Panel has defined several elements involved in teaching reading. Although these elements can be developed in isolation, it is not necessary to teach them in a sequence. In fact, many of the elements can and must be developed simultaneously. Comprehension, which is considered the highest order of reading skills, is directly dependent upon the child's level of experience and language development. Language development is the product of many different experiences within the family and in the community. The more the family engages in a number of activities, the wider the language development will become.

NATIONAL READING PANEL CRITERIA

The National Reading Panel identified the following elements in developing reading skills:[3]

Phonemic Awareness

In a modern society, phonemic awareness surrounds a young child. What can be done to reinforce this concept? The child learns that speech is made up of words and that words are made up of sounds.

Phonics

Is phonics necessary to early reading for all children? Phonics is the identification of the sounds of speech with the letters that represent them. A true phonetic spelling system would have a one-to-one match of sounds to letters. In English, forty-four sounds are represented by 196 combinations of the twenty-six letters of the Roman alphabet. Once the printing press was invented, we froze English spelling using an inadequate alphabetic system.

There have been a number of attempts to reform the system. Alexander Graham Bell and his father, Melville Bell, invented a true phonetic alphabet. Each letter was designed so that it actually told the reader how to make the sound. It was called *Visible Speech*. Unfortunately, the publishing houses did not adopt it even though the Bells did publish some books using their alphabet. George Bernard

Shaw left a considerable portion of his fortune to reforming English spelling. Sir James Pitman developed an Initial Teaching Alphabet (ITA) that was close to a one-to-one match of sounds to letters.[4] In order to develop his theories, he had a number of early reading books published in this alphabet. However, since the publishing industry never accepted his alphabet, there were a limited number of books available. He assumed that once the child learned to read with the ITA, it would be a simple matter to transfer to traditional spelling.

Fluency

What steps can encourage children to read fluently? How can reading for pleasure be developed in young children? Young readers often model their reading after the pattern of family reading. If newspapers, magazines, and books are in the home, children have a better chance of becoming good readers.

Once encoding and decoding skills are achieved, the new reader must become fluent in reading. Fluency is often accomplished by children reading series books on their own because they are eager to be engaged and entertained.

The current interest in the Harry Potter series is an example of a series that can engage and increase the child's reading fluency. *Harry Potter* is interesting in that it is not only a book but also a complete structure of modern communications systems with audio books, videotapes, DVD, films, and computer components. The use of all of these media reinforces the reading skills. However, there is also the danger that a young person will be content with just the audiotapes or video version of the story. Young people develop fluency because they read these books that are relatively easy for them to read for pleasure.

Vocabulary Building

How do children learn new vocabulary? What is a rich environment that leads to vocabulary building? Throughout our lives, we constantly increase our vocabulary. Certainly in technical areas we must find ways to understand the new technologies that come into our daily speech.

In the early days of space exploration, television provided excellent examples of how to increase vocabulary and comprehension skills. Major newscasters were the public's teachers using complex animated illustrations of how the Russian and American spacecraft docked. Although these were aimed at the general public, they were also marvelous teaching programs for both vocabulary expansion and comprehension. Mr. Rogers interviewed astronauts and was able to ask questions that young children had, such as how do you use the bathroom in space. His talks with astronauts enabled very young children to have an understanding of space terminology and events.

Comprehension

How do we develop in children the logical processes that enable them to read with comprehension? As Richard Allington has pointed out, we are not doing a good job in the upper elementary grades of developing good logical comprehension skills in many children. One of the best ways to increase comprehension is perhaps team learning, where learners are working together to solve problems and create projects. The give-and-take of discussions among their peers and the coaching by teachers and other adult experts expand their knowledge and world.

NOTES

1. I had a number of personal discussions with John Henry Martin as he developed the "Writing to Read" programs. I acted as a consultant as he developed the program.

2. I was Ms. McGinnis's special assistant and clinical supervisor when she was writing her book on the Association Method. Mildred A. McGinnis, *Aphasic Children: Identification and Training by the Association Method* (Washington, D.C.: Alexander Graham Bell Association for the Deaf, 1963).

3. National Reading Panel, *Teaching Children to Read: An Evidence-Based*

Assessment of the Scientific Research Literature on Reading and Its Implications for Reading Instruction (Washington, D.C.: National Institute of Child Health and Human Development, National Institutes of Health, 2000).

4. I exchanged a series of letters with Sir James Pitman as he introduced his ideas into the United States.

FIVE

Literacy and Technology

The change from atoms to bits is irrevocable and unstoppable.

—Nicholas Negroponte

Technology enables the learner to use text, images, audio information, and computer information interchangeably. How can curriculum be designed so that it takes advantage of the associative powers of these stimuli? The young child will have watched thousands of hours of television prior to her first day of school. This small digital window in children's homes brings in an expanded view of the real world and enlarges their world. Although television is a facsimile of the real world, it is almost interchangeable with the real world. For many young children, Elmo, Big Bird, Mr. Rogers, Barney, or any number of other television characters promote positive learning experiences. They are a part of the daily lives of young children.

Many young children watch five or six hours of television daily. Although there are positive images on television, there unfortunately are also pictures and sounds of war, violence, murder, and mayhem. We must understand that television, audio recordings, and video games are part of the young child's environment that shapes his understanding of the world.

Most children have played video and computer games. Almost every child has experiences with telephones. They have talked with grandmothers across town and even across the continent and around the world.

When one of my grandsons was three and lived in another state, he learned to speed dial me. The first time he did this, I was sure that it was a wrong number. I asked the little kid with whom he wanted to talk, and he replied, "You, Grandpa! Why would I call you if I didn't want to talk to you?" Children grow up with the technology, and its operation is second nature to them.

Children observe technology in action, whether it is in ordering a Big Mac or selecting their favorite toy at Toys "R" Us. The family that uses technology—from reading newspapers, magazines, and books to computer access and games—creates a climate for literacy. Just as Shakespearean plays are different when performed on television as opposed to being acted upon a stage, a book is different when read in an electronic form than in the traditional print or bound book. However, it is no less reading.

A critical element with all learners is that there is a dialogue between the adult and the child, whether it is on television or in the reading of the book. The crucial issue is: what did the expresser want to tell you, the receiver? It is important that children learn to critically use information sources. Children and users of all forms of information must critically examine and understand how different mediums are used.

Certain things are so dangerous that students should not handle them until they have learned safe ways to use them. For example, chemistry classes in high school laboratories report a number of serious accidents each year. Some chemistry-training programs allow students to simulate experiments on the computer. Once the students have demonstrated in the simulation that they know the procedures, then and only then do they deal with actual chemical substances.

Today, sophisticated driver simulations are used to teach driver education. Just as the pilot training simulators can give pilots hours of success in simulation systems, students learning to drive can experience very lifelike simulations. There are even inexpensive computer programs that teach driving and piloting skills.

The challenge is to use the right technology at the right time. Technology should never be used just for the sake of technology. Technology should increase the learning experience for the learner.

Six

Literacy, Curriculum, and School Achievement

> The most significant learning technologies are wearable glasses and electric lights since they enable people to read at any time and throughout their lives.

> —Barbara Tuchman

The key to intellectual growth and development ever since Gutenberg invented the printing press has been universal reading and writing. Books and libraries led to the creation of schools for the masses. Andrew Carnegie's concept of free public libraries in the United States of America was equal and comparable to Horace Mann's concept of free public schools for all children. Thomas Jefferson felt the greatest failure in his life was that he was unable to persuade the state of Virginia to create a universal elementary school for all children. To take full advantage of libraries and schools, individual learners had to master literacy.

As recently as 1950, the key to all formal education was to be able to read print-based books and have access to libraries. However, since 1950, new electronic information resources have competed with books and expanded our ability to store and retrieve knowledge. Consequently, television, audio programs, and now computers compete for the time available for reading.

Barbara Tuchman, the distinguished historian, said that the two greatest technologies ever invented for education were wearable glasses and the electric light. Together, they allow users to read throughout their lifetimes and at any place and at any time. There is a finite amount of time available for each individual to learn and use stored information resources. Tuchman's answer was brilliant, in that she identified the crucial element in all learning, time on task. Any technology that allows us to more efficiently spend time on task will increase our ability to learn.

Herbert Simon, a Nobel Laureate in computer science from Carnegie Mellon University, once said, "Data bases are like the *New York Times*, they contain a lot of information. Much of that information is not what you are searching for, but you develop a management system that allows you to effectively search out the section you want. If you want only to read the *New York Times* editorials you know how to locate them."[1]

We are developing the tools that allow us to efficiently search and retrieve the electronic information that we want. The observations of both Tuchman and Simon are crucial as we think about digital technologies. Tuchman's observations indicate universal access and Simon emphasizes the need to efficiently mange information.

We are raising our children in a multimedia environment. Before writing and books, information was carried in songs, dance, and storytelling. Today, the average person has a cornucopia of information readily available at home. In fact, we live in a vast ocean of information resources. It is essential that young people learn how to manage this large amount of available information.

The "I Have a Dream" speech of Dr. Martin Luther King, Jr., is one example of this expanded multimedia approach. Any student can obtain text, audio, and video formats of Dr. King's speech. A student might wish to use all three formats. We live in a sea of data that can, if organized, become information. The information can become knowledge and, over time, that knowledge can become wisdom. Libraries and books have always contained more information than any single person could assimilate.

Shakespeare is available on videotape, DVD, and interactive multimedia packages. In fact, selected scenes can be viewed with different actors portraying Hamlet or other characters and comparisons can be made. More people saw the BBC television versions of the plays than have seen Shakespearean theater plays in the long history of such theater. One computer version of Hamlet allows the students to create their own sets and costumes.

Ken Burns's television documentary on the Civil War has revitalized our understanding of the issues in the Civil War. *Roots,* when it first aired, outsold every book on the Civil War in many bookstores. Traditional high school courses and textbooks took at most a week to consider this major event in American history. Textbooks devoted no more than three to five pages. Spin-offs from Burns's *Civil War* created works directed toward the influence of the war on communications, transportation, medicine, and social welfare. The concept of the state being responsible for the disabled veteran was a direct influence of the Civil War. Communications and medical technologies expanded greatly as a result of the war. The new technologies allow for nonlinear examinations of events and places.

We often hear that knowledge is doubled every eighteen months and, therefore, people must somehow learn to assimilate that knowledge. No single person can learn that much. The question is not how to assimilate it, but how to manage and organize it. We are bombarded with information on all sides; therefore, we must teach users how to find and critically assess it. True comprehension means a wise use of knowledge and how to organize it so that it is relevant to our goals and objectives. We must learn to critically use television, Internet sources, books, and libraries.

The United States of America was a leader in the concept of universal education for all children. Congress and the administration have reiterated this concept in the current federal legislation of No Child Left Behind.[2] Literacy is the foundation for success in schools. What literacy means in a digital age is the ability to analyze critically all that is read, viewed, and listened to. Literacy means that a person can use many forms of receptive and expressive symbol systems.

The comprehension of coded symbols is partially dependent upon the actual sensory experiences of the learner. What knowledge does the user bring to the literacy experience? For example, a two-dimensional black-and-white picture of an elephant cannot depict for a four-year-old the reality of an elephant. A full-color motion picture of the animal will add to the child's understanding. Attending a circus where they see and hear elephants or visiting elephants in a zoo gives children a better understanding of elephants. Standing on the curb when a three-ton elephant comes down the street gives the child yet another dimension of the concept of elephant. The young infant begins to observe and relate to the sensory experiences in the environment. They associate symbolic codes for the things within their environment.

As the child learns to use stored images, sounds, and text, vicarious learning can stand in for actual sensory learning. Today, with virtual computer simulations, the boundaries between actual and stored experiences are becoming blurred. For example, a Navy pilot in a flight simulator can practice landing a jet airplane on the deck of an aircraft carrier and experience almost the exact things he or she would in real life. The challenge for educators is when to use such learning resources efficiently.

For example, the cost benefit of training a Navy pilot to land on a carrier deck is obvious. Trial and error with a multimillion-dollar machine, much less the lives of the pilot and the crew aboard ship, indicates that we should spend large sums of money developing a simulator. In public education, driver simulators are a similar example of cost-effective uses of technology. The handling and development of simulated chemical reactions is another area that can be a cost-effective learning experience. Obviously, the Navy pilot, the high school driver, and the chemistry student need to eventually perform in the real world, but it is cost effective to use simulations to develop skills.

As teachers and student learn through technology, we will better understand the technology needed for certain content areas. Music composition and conducting has long been taught using music simulators. If I play an oboe, I can actually play along with the National Symphony Orchestra in my practice. The student learning to compose or conduct can create an orchestra that plays his compositions.

It is more important than ever that all forms of literacy be understood and used in creating high-quality curriculum. Audio, video, and computer resources are extensions of the literacy synergy of symbols and codes. Achievement in academic areas is enhanced by high-quality curriculum.

Just as there are very few great musical composers, I believe there are few great curriculum developers. Curriculum development in the digital age requires a creative team that is composed of content specialists, technologists, editors, film producers, webmasters, and assessment specialists. The team leader and team must be able to understand the various needs of the learners who will use the final product. They must build alternative pathways through the curriculum that meet the abilities and needs of the learners. It is a difficult and complex task, one that we are learning how to create in the digital age.

We have adapted technology to learning in the military and industry because we have specific tasks that we want the student to learn. A Navy pilot must learn to take off and land from the deck of an aircraft carrier. The milling machine operator must be able to meet the tolerances of the milling project set by the industry. The learning goals are broader and more complex in teaching reading and literacy skills. However, we have elements that we can target our product toward and assessment benchmarks to evaluate our success in teaching those benchmarks.

The following chapters detail the criteria for using a mix of text, images, and sounds in creating engaging curriculum. They also develop a strategy for assessment of academic achievement.

NOTES

1. Personal conversation and meeting with Herbert Simon at Carnegie Mellon University on a federal site visit.

2. No Child Left Behind is the current version of the major Elementary and Secondary Education Act Public Law 107–110.

SEVEN

Learning in the Twenty-First Century

Education is learning what you didn't even know you didn't know.

—Ralph Waldo Emerson

AMERICAN SCHOOLS 2010

The first decade of the twenty-first century has the potential for significant changes in the ways Americans think about and offer all children a chance to be all they can be. It is the best of times and the worst of times. Never before have we had the tools that can reach every child with programs that meet their learning needs. That is the good news. The bad news is that our schools are crumbling down around our teachers and students. Although we have examples of exemplary new schools, most of our school facilities are antiquated and in disrepair, especially in our central cities. We have moved forward in providing access to the Internet, but we are still not completely wired.

Surveys of high school students tell us that they have greater access to the Internet at home and in community centers than they do in schools. Current school buildings are too large and too outdated to meet the needs of all students and to use the telecommunications resources available. Teachers and students need the best possible resources to enhance the learning of every child. We also need access to learning technologies in every student's home. We cannot remain prisoners of time and space. We must strive to make the world our classroom for every child.

There is a critical shortage of teachers who are prepared to use the new technologies. Many high school students feel they are experts on Internet and that, although some of their teachers are at best moderate experts in its use, most teachers are beginners. We need teachers who are competent in content areas, understand theories of learning, and can engage all students.

THE VISION

In our efforts to leave no child behind, we must acknowledge that we are rapidly developing a bifurcated school system through the digital divide.[1] The National Telecommunications and Information Administration (NTIA) in the U.S. Department of Commerce has issued two reports on the digital divide indicating that poor schools are falling further behind affluent communities and schools. Even so, there are positive examples around the nation, such as Union City, New Jersey, which has adopted and infused technology in all aspects of its school system. However, there are poor systems that are operating in buildings that do not have the electric wiring to use technology.

The truly disadvantaged learner in the twenty-first century will be the learner without technology. Technology can go into the most isolated environment. There is no excuse other than the failure of the community to have the will to use technology to ensure that all children have the best possible learning environment. It is our choice; even in a time of retrenchment and budget cuts, we must provide a technology-based education for every child.

By 2010, the nation will have developed local, regional, and national digital libraries of learning materials as a subset of the Internet. Such libraries will have core operating systems that allow for the placement of organized courseware developed by either commercial or public-sector developers.

Many public-sector developments will be free or inexpensive. All materials will be billed on a user-fee basis, that is, either a universal subscription basis or a direct fee-for-use basis. The core operating system of the digital library will allow for the storage of all materials within the library and arrange for the distribution and billing according to the users' needs. School systems can subscribe to the library, and all students within the school system can access materials and/or individual learners can subscribe to the digital library resources. In 2000, the fundamental principles of such a digital library system was under development through the joint venture of the digital library initiative funded through the National Science Foundation with assistance from the U.S. Department of Education, NASA, and the Department of Defense.

How Will It Work?

An individual student operating from anywhere will be able to access the digital library through his school and personal access codes. Multimedia lessons will be available and the students will have access to the search information on the Internet to further their lessons. A teacher will mentor the students as they progress through the lessons. Students will individually and in teams produce project-based reports that demonstrate their knowledge and skills. Not all learning will be individual study, but will include teaming with other students, small-group discussions, and large classroom lectures when appropriate.

Learning will be managed through the Individual Student Learning Plan. Both human and technical resources will be available to students when they appear to be having difficulties. Interactive tutorial programs will be available through computer applications. Most, if not all, learning will be voice activated, that is, the student will enter the computer learning programs by natural voice input, asking questions, and making responses to computer-generated questions.

Some worry that e-learning and independent study from a distance will isolate students. They also question whether the work will be done by the student or by someone else. Could the student hire an expert to do the course and then take credit for the work? We know the Internet has opened the world up to plagiarism because it is easy to clip and paste other people's work. We need to teach students ethical and moral ways to use technology. Experience has shown that there are ways to overcome these fears. Research on the Star Schools projects found that students felt they were in a large class even though on site they might have been alone or with three to six other students. They often felt that they had more direct contact with teachers than in regular classes.

Educators and schools must learn to use technology wisely as other professions have done. If you were having chest pains and went to a cardiologist who had trained in 1960 and he said, "I'm only going to use a stethoscope and a blood pressure measurement system," you would probably seek another doctor. If he said that treadmills, CT scans, and laser technologies were just not of interest to him and that he couldn't be bothered with learning to use them, you would go to another doctor. In fact, if his office and support staff looked as it did in the 1960s, you would go somewhere else, no matter how much you personally liked the doctor. If he treated you as he would have in the 1960s and you died, your family might even sue the doctor for malpractice.

Why then are we so willing to tolerate teachers who fail to use learning technologies? Shouldn't we ask questions of why teachers fail to provide the learning resources needed in a modern digital society? In fact, it has been said that if teachers of 1900, 1930, or 1950 were to come back to their classrooms, they would not find anything different. They would be able to take up in the same manner they did when they taught.

Why does it take so long for education to change? We have not yet achieved universal literacy in the world. It is as if we were in the 1700s when cheap books became available for learners and teachers. The late Doc Howe, when he was the U.S. Commissioner of Education, was asked why teachers were so slow to adopt new technology. He replied that they had not been taught through technology.

Teachers often teach based upon the patterns and experiences they have had in their own learning experiences. In teacher preparation courses, technology was often one course late in their program. He opined that if they had been taught without books and had a similar course on the values of books in education, they would adopt books in about the same ratio as they adopt technology.

The challenge is how to bring teachers into the digital age. They will need to learn a new pattern of teaching where the learner is the focus of the school. Technology does that; it concentrates the learning and teaching partnership on the learner rather than the teacher. It brings together learning resources so that they are available to the learner. Digital technology especially allows the learner to expand and break up the materials to be learned. It can demonstrate for the learner complex scientific reactions and allow the learner to examine such things at her own pace. Digital technology allows for the teacher to organize for the learner a wide range of experiences. It is both a micro and macro window on the world.

The teacher who fails to bring technology to the desk of the learner is failing to practice the high calling of teaching. Teachers must become accountable.

The digital age has already changed the emphasis of learning to focus on the learner and not the teacher. It will ultimately change the nature of education and redesign schools, as we know them. We already see evidence of these changes. It is possible for every learner to have an individualized learning profile that can bring him the needed human and technical resources. Some of these resources might be individual tutors, others could be large class lecture systems, and others will bring us technical resources.

Who Will Develop the Materials for the Digital Library?

A combination of public and private developers will create the materials needed for the digital library. The Core Operation System (COS) will track and use and copyright payments to all relevant parties. For example, the entire library of materials of the National Geographic Society will be accessible in the library, as would the entire library of other publishing houses. Teachers and students would have a vastly expanded universe of materials, and they

would pay a minimum for use of such materials. Government-pro-
duced materials at the local, state, or federal levels would also be
retrievable from such a library system. The cost of developing
high-quality multimedia materials is increasing, but this form of
distribution will ensure widespread use and will distribute costs
accordingly.

Development

The American government has recognized the need for support
of technological infrastructures since the middle of the 1800s. In
1858, because of economies of scale, the federal government in-
vested in the American Printing House for the Blind. In effect,
blind children were entitled to the same textbooks as sighted children. However, the market in education of books for blind children
was so small that the government created the American Printing
House for the Blind (APH). APH's mission is to transform books
into a usable form for the child who is blind. Any textbook needed
by a blind student was transformed into braille.

By 1958, the government determined that children who are deaf
are entitled to view educational films available to all children;
therefore, they created the Captioned Films for the Deaf program
that now includes entertainment and educational materials. The
Captioned Film for the Deaf program has been extended to television programs and the Library of Congress provides a wide range
of recorded books and magazines for people who are blind.

In 1967, the Public Broadcasting Service was established to provide educational materials for schools. The federal government
provides funding for the equipment for PBS and has underwritten
some educational television program production. Recently, the E-
Rate legislation has provided money for schools to pay for telecommunications equipment and services. These efforts are based upon
the need for economies of scale. The market simply will not support the development of these resources in the private sector. Even
the cable Learning Channel was originally federally supported.

The time and high cost of development of quality programs requires cooperation among various participants from high-tech

companies and academic institutions to distribution systems. Carefully crafted federal development programs can develop the prototypical model for design and development of such materials. These projects must be of sufficient size and scope to ensure careful design and testing of materials before being placed in large-scale use. The federal government should be a major partner in the development of high-quality content materials.

THE SCHOOL

There is an opportunity to develop a new form of excellence. We know that learning occurs twenty-four hours each day. We know that access to the Internet should become universal in homes, schools, and workplaces. We need uniform national requirements that broadband universal access is available to everyone, in homes and throughout communities. In other words, universal broadband services should be the minimum standard for all such services.

This is essential for the learner, but even more so for the teacher. For the teacher to function in a high-tech world, he must be familiar with the resources of the information age. We are experimenting with new forms of housing for teachers. We can build educational parks that include housing, schools, libraries, museums, and community centers.

Because of technology, we no longer need to think of large schools, but can build schools that are small enough for all staff members to know by name every student. The actual school in the educational park will house between 300 and 500 students. Educational parks of the future will have housing for educational staff, digital libraries that bring the world into the classroom, rotating museum exhibits, and community-based recreational facilities, including a community auditorium. Teachers will have subsidized housing within the park. Some housing in the educational park will be available to families of children enrolled in the schools.

These educational parks will operate year round and be open

daily from 7 A.M. to at least 7 P.M. with organized educational programs.

Some educational parks will operate within work environments of business campuses. Enrollment in such programs will be centered on the children of the employees.

THE TEACHER

Every teacher will have on his or her desk a "Teacher's Associate" that provides an educational database with a profile on each learner, cross-referenced to learning standards and learning resources. In addition, the Teacher's Associate can bring into the classroom electronic learning resources that can be used in teaching group lessons and also can be delivered to the individual learner's desk for that student to learn at his own pace. The system has a built-in assessment program so that the progress of each individual learner is measured and available to the teacher in planning and developing the learning of each child. Parents can access this educational utility so that they can interact with the teacher and student in monitoring and planning the educational life of their child. Learning resources will be available 24 hours each day, 365 days a year.

Learners will have their own laptop computers so that they can access the system at school and also from their homes. This educational utility will accumulate the learning of the students from all sources and make it available within their educational profiles.

THE CHILD

Every child will have an individualized education plan that includes clearly defined educational goals and objectives developed with teachers and the families of the child. Daily and weekly assessment and measurement of the child's progress toward these goals will be a part of the system. The electronic resources of the school system will be available to children at all times year round.

Every child will have access to the Internet at home and in the classroom.

Schools will not be the old-fashioned factory-model, assembly-line instructional programs. Because children learn at different rates and in different styles, the teacher will be the mentor and guide of the children as they progress toward their individual goals. Teachers will be general practitioners managing the educational progress of each pupil assigned to them. Rather than being assigned to a specific grade, the teacher will be responsible for working with pupils for at least three years as they mentor the child through the curriculum. Consequently, the teacher must understand a broad range of curricula materials and programs. Children will work in clusters or teams and engage in product-based projects.

Every child will achieve acceptable levels of twenty-first-century literacy within the first year of school. *Literacy* means an adequate spoken vocabulary, reading and writing skills, and digital technology skills. Literacy in its broadest terms is essential for all further learning, which means the ability to both receive and express all forms of human communications.

In the year 2003, 60 percent of American homes have Internet connections. By 2010, every child attending public schools must have access to the Internet both in school and in their homes. For those families who cannot afford such connections, the school system will provide access.

According to Moore's Law, computers double in power every eighteen months and the cost is reduced by 50 percent. Since the first computer in World War II, they have doubled seventy-five times. To put this in greater perspective, the computer you buy off the shelf today for $1,500 is more powerful than a $16,000,000 supercomputer of a little more than a decade ago. We haven't seen anything yet. We are seeing clothes with computers embedded in them, wearable computers that allow the users to see in front of them a screen of information, and our houses are full of a large array of computers. Using the wearable computer, one might attend a conference and meet a person whose name one might have forgotten. The wearable computer would scan the person and provide the name and location of the last personal encounter.

The Age of Imagination: The Age of Mind Extenders

If the nineteenth century was the age of steam that replaced human muscle power, then the twenty-first century will be the age of mind extenders. This means a new and expanded concept of schools. This means we can do what we talked about in the twentieth century of providing individual educational programs that meet the unique needs of every child.

To "be all we can be" will take unusual leadership—leadership that is willing to throw out the old that is no longer relevant and to map out a new concept of learning and teaching. It is a time for high academic standards, but also a time for understanding the needs of the twenty-first century. It is a time to create partnerships among various educational entities, from preschool to graduate school. We are all one system but along the way we have become bifurcated and isolated one from another. We must no longer allow this to happen.

Scientific educational research has told us how to make schools efficient in the twenty-first century. During the 1990s, we have had a number of experimental new school projects. We need to have leaders who can step up and make it work. One such leader might be an industry willing to create a school on its industry campus. Schools started out around the work needs of the farmer. In the twenty-first century, let's create a school around the modern workplace. Such schools have the advantage of having the children and parents working and learning in the same environment. Parents can be a real part of the child's learning experiences.

Let no child be lost because we did not have the will to implement the best that we know with respect to learning. The challenge is up to each of us to bring about a new and better learning environment.

Priorities

Each level of government has a unique and relevant role in the grand partnership for educational quality. The federal government should do those things that require economies of scale and that cannot be effectively funded at state and local levels. This means:

- Federal programs should design, develop, and ultimately operate the National Educational Digital Library.
- Fund long-term development of high-quality courseware for use within the National Educational Digital Library.
- Support, in cooperation with state governments, the creation of staff development programs for both inservice and preservice teachers.

Although the U.S. Constitution left to the states the responsibility for education, the 1983 Secretary of Education, T. H. Bell, shocked the nation with *A Nation at Risk*. A modern society cannot fail to educate all of its children and we cannot allow some states to not prepare teachers. Unfortunately, teacher preparation programs have often not kept pace with the technological development in local schools. Coupled with the teacher shortage, the crisis is of sufficient magnitude that it must be addressed at the federal as well as state level.

- Provide state-approved development of high-technology programs, including the E-Rate technology funding program.
- Provide state demonstration projects of technology applications.

State governments must fund those things that meet essentially statewide needs. State governments can and must develop (again, because of economies of scale) programs that are universally needed throughout a given state. These might be statewide networks that allow the schools to access the National Digital Library, or high-quality teacher preparation programs.

Local governments must provide the leadership for the day-to-day operation of the learning systems needed within their communities. This includes the year-round operation of schools and all electronic learning services within their respective communities.

The learning resources must be available in the homes of every learner as well as in classrooms, libraries, and museums.

FUNDING

Educational funding is undergoing a crisis in the United States. It is ironic that we have an increasing school population, the largest federal investment in education, and a funding crisis. Traditional funding from property taxes has proven to be inequitable. Therefore, funding should be a true partnership among local, state, and federal sources. Direct appropriation is, of course, the most obvious but it has never been a true federal, state, and local partnership.

Only through the Individuals with Disabilities Education Act (IDEA) has the federal government recognized a responsibility for all disabled children. Unfortunately, that legislation has never been fully funded. All other federal funds have been discretionary, that is, targeted funding programs. A fair federal share of educational costs for disabled children would result in a large new federal expenditure of, say, one-third of the cost of K–12 for such children. If this philosophy were accepted for all current school-aged children in school, it would cost $120 billion annually.

The nation is at sufficient risk for this to happen. The 1983 report *A Nation at Risk* implied that we were at sufficient risk, but so far our solutions have been to think only in terms of local and state solutions.

Other forms of funding, such as the E-Rate, are not direct taxation dollars. There are programs that could be tax credits or that could supplement the school tax dollar. Everyone who uses a telephone supports the E-Rate that provided telecommunications resources to K–12 schools.

An educational tax fund could be developed from sales of televisions, cable, and computers that would be devoted to operating and maintaining a National Digital Library and to developing high-quality curriculum materials. A 1 percent tax on all such devices sold could be comparable to the federal highway tax.

A national finance task force should be given one year to come up with a new formula for funding K–12.

ASSESSMENT

From the early days of computers with Donald Bitzer, Patrick Suppes, John Seely Brown, and Alfred Bork, we have dreamed that computers could be the tools that enable us to measure educational outcomes. Originally with mainframe computers, we thought that we would be able to map the elements of a given subject area, organize it, and measure the learners' entrance level skills. Then we would plot a course of study and measure the learners' gains in skills and knowledge. At the completion of the computer-assisted instructional program, we would have assessed progress and gains in skills and knowledge.

For certain skill-centered programs in places like the military and NASA, these dreams materialized. As early as World War II, Link trainers simulated actual pilot training. Today's sophisticated flight simulators allow the pilot to feel and experience simulations of flights from hundreds of airports around the world. The NASA shuttle simulators give astronauts realistic experiences of shuttle flights. These simulators also record the experiences of the trainees.

After the first Gulf War, we debriefed the officers of the participating nations and asked them why they performed so well.[2] The universal answer was that the simulation training they had received made the real task of combat seem like just another experience. The training of astronauts is another example of technology-based training that has all the elements of prior knowledge and increased skills built into the training simulations. The astronauts who repaired the Hubble telescope performed tasks that had never before been conducted in the real world because they had, in effect, overlearned their repair tasks in simulations.

Unfortunately, the military, astronaut, and pilot training worlds can afford the costs of highly developed skill training programs more easily than the general field of K–12 education. We know how to develop such programs, especially for skill development.

We even know how to apply this information to some areas of general education, but we have seldom applied it in sufficient scope and depth to demonstrate increased learning.

Historically, we have a record of technology making a significant difference in education of children. Perhaps the most evaluated program over the years is the computer curriculum. The Jostin Integrated Learning programs have also demonstrated achievement in West Virginia, as well as other places. One of the most interesting aspects of the West Virginia experiment has been that it has been used systematically throughout the state. Its implementation is a planned program moving from the early grades to upper grades. The Waterford Early Reading Program is another program that has had a number of years of systematic scientific research that shows significant learning, if applied consistently. The oldest of computer instructional program, PLATO, is still available in various forms and has demonstrated its value.

The effectiveness of the applications of technology to learning is related to two factors: (1) the design of the courseware and (2) systematic and long-term applications of the technology. Poorly or inappropriately designed software can hinder rather than improve learning. Sporadic uses of the technology can hinder assessment.

Perhaps the most important influence of computer-based learning is that the educational paradigm has shifted from an emphasis on instruction to learning. This means that the learner is the center of the educational process rather than the teacher. The computer has demanded that we examine the entrance-level skills and knowledge of the user and that we can, with sufficiently designed software, monitor the learning progress of every student as they progress through the use of the courseware. Unfortunately, few programs have developed the computer-based management tools that chart the progress of the students. However, the move toward standards and the establishment of the National Educational Technology Standards hold great promise for management software that will allow teachers to assess every child's learning progress.

Gordon Ambach, when he was the chair of the International Educational Assessment program, commented a few years ago that we will need to continue traditional measurements at the same time we develop new measurement techniques that will measure computer and constructionist theories of learning. The Stanford Achievement Test series, ninth edition (SAT 9) and other traditional factual measures of educational skills will still be needed as we develop new measures of critical thinking and problem-solving abilities.

Patrick Suppes's Computer Curriculum Corporation (CCC) programs have demonstrated success in student learning. Dustin Heuston's Waterford Early Reading programs are well researched and documented. Certainly, the military applications and astronaut training, as well as industrial uses of technology demonstrate the efficacy of computer/technology-based learning.

Early Educational Testing Service (ETS) studies of the influence of *Sesame Street* indicated that success could be measured as a factor of time watching the program and age. For example, a three-year-old watching twice as much as a four-year-old would learn at the same level. Other studies of television program such as *3-2-1 CONTACT!*, *Square One TV*, and *The Voyages of the Mimi* clearly indicated that time on task increased learning. Since the 1950s, we have known that "good," well-designed television teaches to the same level as most classroom teachers.

Assessment must, as Gordon Ambach indicated, follow a dual path. We must continue traditional measures and at the same time create product-based assessment and profile assessments of students. We have the power to do data mining and correlation on individual students if we want to. The National Basketball Association has applied it to basketball, and coaches have tons of data on each player. We should be willing to use the same management and assessment systems in teaching core curriculum.

LINGUISTIC DEVELOPMENT

Children growing up in a digital electronic world have both a wonderful and daunting world of experiences. The average two- to five-year-old is one of the greatest consumers of television. Positive programs such as *Sesame Street* and *Mister Rogers' Neighborhood* enrich the child's life and experiences. However, we know that at midnight some five-year-olds are watching television. Television is often violent and antisocial in nature. From the Surgeon General's studies in the 1970s and many other studies, we know that television does influence child growth and development.

In addition to television, video games and books are more likely to be available today than ever before. The worldwide success of the *Harry Potter* series is an interesting and exciting phenomenon. The literacy level of *Harry Potter* is perhaps slightly higher than *The Hardy Boys* and *Nancy Drew*, but the fact that six- to twelve-year-olds are reading *Harry Potter* in unprecedented numbers is a positive factor. I have long believed that this type of literature is what young people cut their teeth on with respect to learning to read for the sheer enjoyment of reading. As readers of *Harry Potter* attest, they read the books over and over again. I tend to see this as a very positive trend among young people around the world. They increase enjoyment and fluency.

Reading specialists are in some ways like the medical professionals in the late 1800s when they argued about bleeding and leeching patients. There is no question that there are several different roads to learning to read. We are experiencing a new surge of people who are classified as advocates of "phonics" as opposed to the "whole language" reading experiences. In fact, in California, some of the most ardent advocates of the whole language approach to reading are now advocates of phonics.

Reading is a secondary linguistic skill that is founded on speech. Consequently, it is difficult to develop good reading skills if your basic linguistic speech and language skills are substandard. We know that the average first grader has approximately a 2,500-word vocabulary, but that the range is from 1,000 to 5,000 words. Unfortunately, we treat all children equally, regardless of the linguistic skill they have when they come to school. A child with a 1,000-word vocabulary functions in kindergarten somewhat on an equal level with the child who has a 5,000-word vocabulary. The child with a 5,000-word vocabulary performs very well when reading instruction begins. He or she has the linguistic framework to quickly associate the spoken word with the written word.

A brief word about the nonphonetic aspects of English spelling is important if we are to understand the development of reading and language skills. At the morphological level, there is more consistency than at the phonological level. Nonetheless, especially for children with a limited vocabulary, the nonphonetic aspects of English cause problems.

Until the printing press, spelling and punctuation were often dependent upon the idiosyncratic style of the scribe who copied the manuscript. However, with the introduction of the printing press, a level of standardization came into spelling and punctuation. Unfortunately, in English, there were many levels of orthographic inconsistencies. There is dual spelling for many sounds. *Ph* and *f* have the same phonetic value and *s* and *c* can also sound the same, as found in words like *suit, cigar, cell,* and *cycle.* Sir James Pitman and George Bernard Shaw both left their fortunes to a crusade to reform English spelling. However, very little has been accomplished in this area. There is some hope that as we develop more effective speech synthesizers and speech analyzers, orthographic reform might slowly emerge.

The philosophy of the U.S. Army recruiting slogan, "Be all that you can be," sums up my understanding of what American education should stand for. Our founding fathers believed that reading and writing were the key to lifelong learning. Once a student was given the key to literacy, the world of knowledge was open to him. In a modern digital world, this means information literacy. Not only will our students need to read and write but they must also be able to navigate the digital world of telecommunications. All teachers must understand developmental linguistics and the fundamentals of mathematics. It is from these foundations that all other knowledge develops.

Science and mathematics are essential elements for elementary schoolchildren and we can introduce such content at very early ages. The adventures of the mind in the information age have never before been as great as they are today. The technology in the average American home has literally hundreds of digital devices that should enable us to provide learners with unbounded learning resources. Part of the challenge is how to best integrate the digital devices of the home with that of the school.

Research on learning and teaching enables us to provide learning environments that meet the needs of every child to master and to achieve a high quality of academic skill and knowledge. Well-designed learning software gives us an opportunity to enable every learner to master the skills and knowledge needed in a complex modern society.

Business adviser Peter Drucker has said that the world needs learners and not knowers. By this, he meant that the world needs people who can find out the information they need and work to solve problems rather than people who have assembled a large number of factoids.

The knowledge base doubles every eighteen months; therefore, the learner must be able to evaluate the new information and either incorporate it into his or her knowledge base or logically reject it. In a simpler time, knowledge was more stable. This does not mean that there are not constants in the world of knowledge today, but it means that learners must have the skills that enable them to use and or reject new knowledge as it emerges. William Shakespeare still is one of the world's best storytellers, Newton's observations are still relevant, but the challenge is how to blend the old truths with the new realities.

NOTES

1. National Telecommunications and Information Administration, *Falling through the Net: Defining the Digital Divide: A Report on the Telecommunications and Information Technology Gap in America* (Washington, D.C.: U.S. Department of Commerce, 1999); National Telecommunications and Information Administration, *Falling through the Net II: New Data on the Digital Divide* (Washington, D.C.: U.S. Dept. of Commerce, 1998).

2. I was on a team of experts that debriefed military personnel in Frankfurt, Germany, after the first Gulf War.

EIGHT

What We Have Learned

We've got to help people understand the value of public education in this country. The quality of life for all of us is tied up in the quality of public education.

—Floretta McKenzie

The passage of the No Child Left Behind federal legislation is in keeping with the growth of federal legislation in the last part of the twentieth century. From 1954 onward, we have brought more and more disenfranchised students into the door of the public schoolhouse. The poor, the disadvantaged, the at-risk, the disabled, and the non-English-speaking students have all found a place in the schoolroom. We are a nation of people who believe all children have a right to a free and appropriate public education.

Nations that do not develop and reform their educational systems so that they give all children access to learning will be left behind in the twenty-first century. Since 1990, the United Nations and the World Bank have had a goal of education for all children. Basically, 161 nations at Jomtiem, Thailand, agreed to at least six years of education for all children.[1] The challenge is how to restructure our schools in the digital age so that they meet our national and international goals.

Just as in the eighteenth century the printing press and availability of cheap books enabled us to create what we know as the modern school, the digital age might cause us to rethink our educational programs. What should public education look like?

THE FEDERAL, STATE, AND
LOCAL PARTNERSHIP

Many nations have realized that there are technology infrastructures that must function from a national level if we are to take advantage of the digital world. In the United States, we must develop a working partnership among the federal, state, and local education agencies. The federal government must finance those things that require economies of scale, such as the telecommunication infrastructure and digital libraries.

The E-Rate is one positive step in the right direction.[2] The federal education departments must create programs that enhance the partnership among federal, state, and local K–12 agencies and institutions of higher education. We must meld our national education system into one system with equality of access and resources for all learners. This does not mean that we will have a federally controlled curriculum, but that we will retain local control with an equality of resources.

The federal government has several prime areas of responsibility:

- The development of telecommunications infrastructures that require large-scale development because of economies of scale.
- Creation of national and regional digital libraries.
- Research, design, and development of digital curriculum programs.
- Creation of appropriate assessment tests based upon research.
- Shared support for targeted populations, such as disabled, disadvantaged, and non-English-speaking learners.
- Preparation of educational staff competent in the uses of digital technologies.
- Technology research in the development of new learning technologies.

Traditional classrooms and teachers will not be replaced, but within a decade they will include Internet resources and there will be e-learning of complete courses. The average learner might study in traditional classrooms supplemented by Internet resources or take entire courses online.

> Some people see things as they are and ask 'why?' I dream of things that never were and ask, 'why not?' " (George Bernard Shaw)

If we develop the education world as envisioned above, what will it look like?

A MODEL ELEMENTARY SCHOOL

This school will take into account all the materials that are available for early education programs. These include television, especially those PBS and cable television programs that are designed for learning. Families also have a wide range of family-oriented resources, from photographs of vacation trips to videos of birthday parties.

Management tools can and should be used to allow for very flexible schedules for students and their families. It is important for a young child to visit a grandparent in Boston even though the child's family might live in San Diego. In fact, the teacher should be able to give the family helpful suggestions about how the visit might be more meaningful for not only the child but also his classmates. It is especially important in these early years that elementary schoolteachers open the classroom to the wider world of childhood experiences. I once had an eight-year-old who was a whiz at creating Web pages. Elementary school is envisioned in a new technology-based digital world as the place where learners can work at their own pace. Technology should respond to the natural inquisitiveness of the child. For example, voice-activated literacy programs can be developed that do the following:

- When the child says a word or sentence, it immediately appears in print on the screen.
- If the child does not understand a word, he can ask the com-

puter to "show me" and the computer will morph the printed word into an object or an animated sequence that represents the action.

- The child, if interested, can ask the computer to transform the print into another language.
- Printed and illustrated stories on the computer can be read aloud to the child at the child's request.
- The child can also read the story aloud and have the computer monitor his reading.

This learning genie can allow the child to ask a number of questions and it will respond in print, spoken language, and/or with illustrations. For example, the child might ask, "Why is the sky blue?" The computer will respond with an age-appropriate answer. There are obvious limits to the stored answers. When this occurs, the computer can provide hints with respect to where that information can be obtained, including telling the child to ask the teacher or parent.

The goal of the first three to four years of this model school will be to establish the foundations for literacy in a digital age. These first years include language development, reading, writing, and the ability to develop expressive ideas through technology as well as receive ideas from technology.

A crucial element of a model elementary school is the technology feedback that can be provided to the learner's parents or childcare givers. Such systems can and should be dial-up programs that give daily reports on a child's progress toward meeting her individual educational goals.

The technology will provide a systematic and logical content for the early years, but the child will progress through the system at his own pace. There will be many individual and small-group learning experiences as well as some large-group class experiences. Children of different ages will be encouraged to work together and to help one another.

As the children move toward the upper elementary and middle school years, they will move into project-based programs.

A MODEL MIDDLE SCHOOL

By the time children move into middle school, they will be empowered to work on their own and to work cooperatively with small groups to do project-based learning. Projects will be clustered in content areas such as science, history, civics, literature, the arts, and sports. Mathematics, reading, and writing will be the tools that the child uses to research and express his solving of problems raised in project-based learning. The learning group may be the child's actual peers in the learner's school, a group of distant learners connected by technology, or the learner's family group. All project-based learning programs will have an expressive element where the team shares what they have learned.

A family might visit the Smithsonian Air and Space Museum in Washington, D.C. In collaboration with the teacher, the student may develop a PowerPoint presentation to share with her class. Crucial to effective learning in project-based education is a management system that carefully monitors each student and assesses the learner's accomplishments. Although the learners can select the content area they are working on at a given time, the management system will monitor the students' progress and ensure that the learners have the required amount of content determined by the curriculum. The management system will keep a detailed profile of each student's work. The management system will have sufficient privacy safeguards.

A MODEL HIGH SCHOOL

Research has demonstrated that a high school should not be more than 1,000 students. In a school this size, it is easy to maintain crowd control. A school this size increases the mixing of all students and avoids divisions based on racial, ethnic, and other groups. The argument for larger schools is economy of scale and wider ranges of course offerings. These arguments can be countered by the effective uses of technology and distance resources.

The construction of a new school today should include the concept of a community-wide center that includes common facilities used by the parks, recreation departments, the public library, and the school. All playing fields, theaters, gyms, and food services should be open to the community.

If possible, there should be homes built within the community school area that can become housing for teachers and administrators. The school should become a lifelong learning resource for the community that operates from 7:00 A.M. to 10:00 P.M. every day throughout the year. Central to the school is the digital public library hub that is open to the school and the community.

Management of student learning and professional resources in a computer-based learner management system that allows for the creation of individualized education plans and programs for every student. Students shall have flexible learning times that allow them to be assessed based upon both individual achievement and team-produced products. A core of content shall reflect the state academic standards. Learners successfully achieve proficiency in meeting these standards by performance-based testing.

Learners are encouraged to engage in team-building activities, such as sports, theater, dance, music in bands and orchestras, and scientific teams and experiments. Learners have flexible time schedules so that they can reasonably be expected to make significant contributions to their team projects and efforts.

In 1996, the U.S. Department of Education funded the development of a virtual high school through the Concord Consortium of Massachusetts.[3] The number of high school students taking credits jumped from 700 in the first year to 3,000 annually in the fourth year. The number of different courses offered rose from 27 to 150. More than a dozen states have created virtual high school programs. The Star Schools projects that began in 1988 now have more than two million students enrolling annually in a wide range of technology-based, distance-learning classes in elementary, middle, and high school programs. Especially beneficial has been the development at the high school level of foreign language and advanced placement courses. Many rural communities simply do not have the resources to attract teachers for these subjects.

MANAGEMENT

The principal, counselors, and teachers work with individual learners and their parents to develop an individualized education plan that is monitored by all parties involved. The principal will review with staff the weekly progress of each student toward the learner's objectives.

Teachers

We have often claimed that teachers are learning coaches and not the "sage on the stage," but we have seldom implemented such coaching situations. Teachers must be professional in their content area, technologically competent, and willing to truly work with learners and teams to reach their stated objectives. They will encourage learners to participate in local, regional, and national competitions. Teachers will teach some formal classes, but no class will exceed twenty students, and teachers will have no more than twenty students that they are responsible for monitoring.

Community

The businesses, public agencies, universities, and nonprofit agencies within the community will develop internships and other working relations with the school and students. To the extent possible, every learner in the high school will have a community mentor who will informally and formally work with the learner during his or her high school career.

Learners

Each student in the school will have a signed contract that details his goals and objectives and the human and technical resources available to him to meet his stated goals. Formal coursework will be related to his goals and objectives, as will team and other group activities. Reasonable timelines and steps toward reaching such goals will be detailed and revised periodically.

A typical schedule for our sample student—for example, Jane—might be:

- Jane's objective is to eventually work in the area of children's programs as teacher, librarian, pediatrician, or social worker.
- MWF 7:00 A.M. to 10:00 A.M.—Internship at the local Head Start Program.
- MTWTFSS as needed—Online Internet course in French literature at home.
- TT 1:00 to 2:00 P.M.—Formal introductory course in biology supplemented by online resources.
- MTWTF 2:00 to 3:00 P.M.—Gym and lifetime recreational sports.
- MWF 10:00 to 12:00 P.M.—English composition and literature.
- MTWTF—Online mathematics courses as needed.
- TT 3:00 to 4:00 P.M.—Civics and American history supplemented by online resources in the library.
- Random scheduling as needed in order to mentor her science research project on early child growth and development. Organize with other team members the study of early development in language skills of three- and four-year-olds.
- TT 5:00 to 6:00 P.M.—Orchestra practice; Jane plays the oboe.
- TT 7:00 to 8:00 P.M.—Play practice; Jane has a part in this year's school play. She is also free to use any of the school resources from seven in the morning until ten in the evening. The central community resources, that is, recreational facilities, food services, and library are open year round.
- Daily workouts and practice for her sports activities.

TECHNOETHICS

When new technologies are introduced, the creators and early users are often obsessed with the technology just for the sake of technology. Society eventually accepts the benefits and the negatives of a technology. For example, the automobile greatly increased human mobility, but with a cost in lives, disabilities, property damage, and air pollution.

With the introduction of each new technology, there is always a gain and loss. Society must decided how to use that technology for its benefit and how to regulate the technology for the well-being of the society. I remember talking in Geneva with Soviet scientists at the beginning of the personal computer explosion. They were concerned with the ease of desktop publishing, e-mail and, eventually, Internet connectivity. Their fears were justified with respect to their society. The new information resources did much to make their society more open.

Computers and telecommunication resources are mind and memory extenders. What if, as Ray Kurzweil predicts, we can by 2020 or 2040 download a human brain into the memory of a computer and that brain can learn in the computer? We can, in content areas, create a teaching machine that can enter into Socratic dialogues with a learner. In some ways, this Socratic teacher is more powerful than a live teacher in that it can be programmed so that it has a large instantaneous memory. It might not have the intuitive skills of a live scholar, but it might have as much as the average teacher. Should we then ethically create such tutors?

In distance learning by television or on the Internet, we can serve thousands of learners with master teachers. This inevitably will change the very nature of learning and teaching. In fact, if we look at the education literature of today and compare it to twenty or thirty years ago, we find that education focuses on the learner, whereas in the past it focused on the teacher. Today, we talk about learning strategies; yesterday, we emphasized instructional strategies.

In our development of software, we often emphasize the glitzy nature of 3-D computer animation rather than the pedagogical content. Technoethics demands that we adhere to the best possible content and not the use of technology simply because it is there. Technology can enable us to create learning experiences that provide new insights into knowledge.

NOTES

1. I was a delegate to the 1990 Education for All Conference from the U.S. Department of Education. I created an exhibit booth based upon technology and literacy for the conference.

2. The E-Rate is part of the Telecommunications Act. It authorizes payments to schools through the universal service fund for creating and operating Internet services.

3. Andrew Zucker, Robert Kozma, et al., *The Virtual High School: Teaching Generation V* (New York: Teachers College Press, 2003).

NINE

The Role of the Federal Government in Learning Technologies

I can only say that I view education as the most important subject which we as a people can be engaged in.

Taxes are the way we do together what we cannot do alone.

—Abraham Lincoln

A BRIEF HISTORY OF TECHNOLOGY AT THE FEDERAL LEVEL

The Tenth Amendment to the U.S. Constitution left to the states those things not covered in the U.S. Constitution. Therefore, it was left to the states to create the authority for education. Public education through formal schools was not a high priority in colonial times. Internships and apprenticeships as well as home-based schooling were the common practice. Higher education fared better and was often supported by religious groups.

Thomas Jefferson, the one founding father who was passionate about public education, believed that his founding of the University of Virginia was the most important accomplishment of his life. Although he was proud of the university, his real passion was for universal education for every child for at least four years. He be-

77

lieved that unless the individual members of the population learned to read, write, and calculate, they would not be able to participate in a democratic government. He was disappointed that he did not achieve this in the Commonwealth of Virginia. In this context, he can be considered the first "education president."

The foundations for public education in the United States of America can be found in state constitutions. The only thing that the federal government has traditionally done is insist that public education be fair and equal.

The federal government has had a long and historic part in funding education for certain populations. In 1836, Amos Kendall, the postmaster general of the United States, gave Kendall Green to the federal government to create an elementary school for deaf children. In the 1860s, Gallaudet College, which is still operational today, was created on the green. In 1858, the American Printing House for the Blind (APHB) and Howard University were created. These are special institutions in the federal budget. They remain semiprivate agencies that are funded by the federal government. In 1862, Senator Justin Smith Merrill from Vermont introduced the program that created the land-grant colleges across the nation. The federal government has been in the business of making the playing ground level for all learners.

By World War I, the rural areas were losing their tax base and rural K–12 schools were inadequately funded. The federal government passed what is today the Vocational Education Act, which was designed to provide monies for schools in rural areas. In 1958, the Captioned Films for the Deaf Act was passed to provide equal access to filmed materials to deaf people. In 1965, the Elementary and Secondary Education Act was passed to redress inequities with respect to tax revenues that plagued inner cities. Since 1965, we have seen a series of legislative actions that have been designed to bring all learners—the poor, the disabled, the non-English-speakers, and others—into the mainstream of American education. Research has shown that the more education a person has, the higher the probability that he or she will be a contributor to society rather than dependent upon society. Horace Mann in the mid-

1800s established that everyone could be taxed to support public education because public education was a social benefit.

The American Printing House for the Blind and the Captioned Films for the Deaf programs were the forerunners of learning technology programs at the federal level. The underlying principle is that all learners should have equal access to learning resources. The federal government stepped in to be the mediating force, that is, to make the resources usable by all learners.

Many aspects of technology are best served by economies of scale and, consequently, require extensive and strong federal leadership. For example, it is unreasonable to assume that individual school districts and state agencies can muster the size and scope of funding to create delivery systems that can compete with commercial satellites or other telecommunication distribution systems. Consequently, Congress created the E-Rate under the universal service requirement of the Federal Communications Commission. This concept ensures, among other things, that all telecommunications users have equable and affordable services. For regular telephone services, the rates are about the same whether the user is in a metropolitan high rise or an isolated rural area. Every user paying into the universal service fund brings this about. The E-Rate is a special part of the universal service program that entitles schools to obtain telecommunication rates that are equitable. The E-Rate balances the need for flexibility and allows state and local school systems to negotiate with commercial telecommunications providers for the needed services dictated by the local educational needs and priorities. Economies of scale would indicate that state and regional pacts for services from telecommunication suppliers are effective.

Former South Dakota's Governor William J. Janklow negotiated a statewide system that should be viewed as a viable pattern for other areas.[1] The FCC can and should modify some of the operational aspects of the E-Rate program, but it would be disruptive to place this program in a block grant program. Such a move would be destructive to the quality of telecommunications services needed by American learners. Every learner everywhere should have reasonable access to the Internet. The E-Rate makes this possible and at the same time allows for local control. It is efficient, economical, and entirely consistent with the bipartisan efforts that instituted this program to leave E-Rate's administration at the Federal Communications Commission.

In the 1960s, the U.S. Office of Education funded demonstration projects using mainframe computers. The National Science Foundation funded the development of major science courses. By 1966, the USOE under the leadership of U.S. Commissioner of Education Harold Howe funded experimental children's television programs. The first series funded was *Sesame Street*. This is one of the best success stories of the Department of Education. *Sesame Street* is now in more than 150 countries and co-produced in 21 countries. *Sesame Street* was created prior to the development of the Public Broadcasting Service.

During the last year of the Lyndon B. Johnson administration, the U.S. Office of Education funded the Academy for Educational Development to study the possible impact of technology on learning and teaching. The Nixon administration buried that report but Congress released it as a congressional report. In the 1970s, NASA experimented with ATS-6 and had the cooperation of the U.S. Office of Education in developing content. Edward David, President Nixon's science advisor, created a presidential report on the transfer of NASA space science to domestic programs.[2]

The education section recommended the creation of satellite-based educational digital libraries. When the report went to the president, the Office of Management and Budget (OMB) considered the recommendations too costly to implement. One by-product was the creation of the National Telecommunications and Information Administration (NTIA) in the Department of Commerce. A major part of the NTIA programs was originally in the Office of Libraries and Learning Technologies at the old U.S. Office of Education. When the Department of Education was created, these programs were transferred to the Department of Commerce in the expectation that they would be eliminated. Since the early 1970s, this program has supplied equipment for public television stations.

In 1982 the Reagan Administration folded all the technology programs—that is, library programs, television programs, basic skills computer programs, and museum programs—into the Education Consolidation and Improvement Act on the assumption that states would continue this development. Education Secretary T. H. Bell used his discretionary funds and funded some planning and demonstration technology programs. Project SLATE was designed to foster statewide planning for the use of computers and Project BEST was designed to demonstrate effective uses of technology in learning and teaching. The 1982 legislation effectively consolidated all technology programs into a block grants program.

It was not until 1988 (Table 9.1) that the Star Schools program began once again to build a place in the U.S. Department of Education for technology.[3] Unfortunately, from 1982 until 1988, there was a minimum learning technology program at the department. This was a crucial time for the development of such programs. The lack of national leadership severely curtailed the development of school library programs and technology programs.

The passage of Title III of ESEA and the Telecommunication Act with E-Rate gave American schoolchildren a new lease on the advantages that technology can offer learners. The Department of Education desperately needs an assistant secretary for technology to provide national leadership to make these resources available to all children. All of Title III of ESEA needs to be modified and fully funded. It is a balance of national programs and provides for the flexibility and freedom needed by state and local agencies. The national section of Title III was never funded for digital libraries.

In the last forty years, consolidation of educational programs has

Table 9.1   Star Schools Budget Summary

FY88	$19,148,000	FY96	$23,000,000
FY89	$14,399,000	FY97	$30,514,066
FY90	$14,813,000	FY98	$34,000,000
FY91	$14,417,000	FY99	$45,000,000
FY92	$18,412,000	FY00	$50,550,000
FY93	$22,777,000	FY01	$59,318,000
FY94	$25,944,000	FY02	$27,520,000
FY95	$25,000,000	FY03	$27,341,120
TOTAL	$452,153,186		

always meant a disaster for library and technology programs. Libraries and digital technologies are essential to a well-developed school system. Their costs require the economies of scale that only the federal government can afford.

Those who fail to learn from past mistakes are doomed to repeat them. Shall we deny the learners and teachers of America this greatest resource since the printing press? Not since Gutenberg's invention has a technology been developed that has the potential for radically changing the nature of learning and teaching. As a nation, we eventually adopted the Jeffersonian concept of universal education for all. Our universal education system has dominated the world in educational concepts irrespective of international achievement tests. We are the nation of people who believe that every child can achieve to his or her fullest ability and that, in doing so, we enrichen our society. The G.I. Bill of Rights extended that promise to higher education for an entire World War II generation. We are the nation that is proud of the concept that "No child should be left behind."

We must extend the vision of learning technology for anyone, any place, and at any time through the Internet to every learner in America. It requires a strong and committed leadership at the federal level. There must be an assistant secretary in the U.S. Department of Education for technology. Whether the program emerges as a block grant or a balanced program, it requires such leadership.

A MODEL TWENTY-FIRST CENTURY LEARNING TECHNOLOGY LEGISLATION

Whereas the world of the twenty-first century is dominated by the digital revolution, it is imperative that the nations of the world create a new and dynamic model of education. A school system that is dominated by the uses of technology in the home, the school, and the workplace must expand into the total world of the child. Technology has made the world the classroom. Based upon the growing development of the knowledge resources, the secretary shall appoint a National Learning Technology Advisory Board to review the use of technology in learning and teaching at all levels. The board shall have at least one representative from early childhood, special, elementary, secondary, and postsecondary education, and representatives from the hardware industry, software industry, and a computer science specialist. The board shall meet at least twice annually or more often as determined by the board and the secretary.

The Board

The purpose of the board is to provide the nation with (1) policy advice with respect to learning and teaching technology resources and (2) oversee the general administration of the twenty-first-century technology programs supported by the federal government.

Administration

The secretary shall appoint an assistant secretary to administer the technology programs supported by the U.S. Department of Education. This assistant secretary shall coordinate the actions of this program with other programs in the Department of Education. In addition, this program shall collaborate with the National Science Foundation, the Department of Labor, the Department of Commerce, and the NASA administrator of education in the creation of a program of national learning technology resources.

Section 1: Learning Technology Flexibility Program

This section shall provide monies to state education agencies that have developed an approved plan for a statewide program of technology. Funds may be used for those areas of highest need as determined by state and local authorities. Applied technologies under this program shall be compatible with national digital libraries and other technical standards as may be applied. Funds under this section shall be allocated based upon a state-approved plan and the number of children enrolled in schools. For the purposes of this section, $1,000,000,000 shall be allocated among SEAs and LEAs.

Section 2: Educational Digital Library

2.1   The secretary in conjunction with other agencies of the government shall initiate the development of a core integrated technology system, a series of national digital libraries, for pre-K–graduate school. The core integrated system will be designed so that publicly or privately developed materials may be retrieved from the library on a subscription-fee basis or on a just-in-time of need fee basis. For the purpose of this section, $25,000,000 is authorized annually.

2.2   The secretary shall fund the development of content cores that can be used by the National Digital Library. For example, there may be core strands in elementary science, graduate level microbiology, English literature, and other high-need content areas. The secretary in conjunction with the board shall determine the content areas of greatest need. Procurements under this section must be of sufficient size, scope, and duration that the highest quality products are developed. The secretary shall encourage the joint development of private and public entities capable of creating high-quality curriculum packages. For the purposes of this section, $20,000,000 shall be available annually.

Section 3: Professional Development

The U.S. Secretary of Education's estimate of the shortage of teachers over the next decade indicates that the majority of teachers will be replaced and new teachers will make up the core of the teaching profession at all levels. This represents both an opportunity and a major crisis. New and better ways of creating competent teachers is essential if we are to maintain the standard of living we now enjoy.

3.1   The secretary shall develop nationwide new ways to prepare teachers to teach using technology. It is essential that new teachers be able to use the information technologies available throughout the world. For the purposes of this section, $750,000,000 will be available.

3.1.1   Integral to every teacher preparation program is adequate hardware and software that enables teachers to use the best that is available in their own classrooms. Prior to making a grant for content development in teacher preparation, the secretary shall ensure that sufficient technologies are available to both teachers and students.

3.1.2   Teacher preparation programs will be designed to take full advantage of the technology resources available. Teacher preparation programs will be designed to reflect the best research on learning and teaching. Teacher preparation programs will emphasize among other things an in-depth understanding of phonetics and linguistics.

3.2   For inservice preparation of teachers already in the classroom, a series of continuing programs shall be developed. For the purposes of this section, $150,000,000 will be available.

3.2.1   A web-based program will be developed that can be individually programmed to meet the specific needs of a teacher.

3.2.2   An intern and mentoring program will be developed that matches teachers with master teachers and provides them an opportunity to model their teaching after master teachers.

Section 4: Research and Evaluation

Teachers require in the information age the tools that can assess the progress of students and provide research data on the effectiveness of a learning strategy. Projects under this section shall (1) develop learning management tools, (2) design evaluation procedures, (3) chart individual learning patterns, and (4) provide guidelines with respect to the effectiveness of technology-based learning. For the purpose of this section, $250,000,000 is made available.

At a time when large federal programs are not fashionable, we are suggesting that the American system is in a crisis and, therefore, we cannot afford not to expend these resources. We further note that in the age of technology we should treat the educational systems as pre-K through graduate school. The technologies allow us to take advantages of scale and to repurpose content for different grade levels.

How does legislation get passed? The administration can draft legislation and submit it to Congress. Congress can initiate a piece of legislation and present it to the appropriate committee. Citizens who feel strongly about issues can lobby their senators and congressmen to introduce legislation. The legislation for the disabled came about through the actions of parents seeking appropriate school placement for their children. When they failed to get satisfaction at the local and state levels, they went to the federal level.

In 1967, the U.S. Office of Education's budget for the education of handicapped children was $37 million; today, it is more than $12 billion. This is an example that grassroots efforts do work and that Congress and administrations do respond to the national needs. Patria Forsythe, mother of a deaf son, and Elizabeth Boggs, mother of a mentally disabled son, worked long and hard to get the legislation that now ensures disabled people in all walks of life receive fair treatment. The genius of our government is that determined people can move mountains and get things done. Sometimes it is slow and sometimes it appears that nothing is happening. Sometimes we even take two steps forward and one step backward. Nonetheless, articulate and concerned people can get things done. In the world of technology, the economies of scale require that we provide the infrastructure at the federal level. That means monies for the development of world-class curriculum.

DIGITAL GENERATION

If you observe your children and grandchildren, have you ever wondered why they have not had to have technology literacy courses? The standing joke is if you can't program your VCR, get an eight-year-old to do it. They have cell phones glued to their ears and know how to tweak every possible digital fantasy from them. They have mastered video games and computers without a second thought. It all comes natural to them because they live in a sea of electronic digital gadgets. Give the average four-year-old a battery-operated toy and watch how fast he or she can put the batteries in the right place and get it to work.

There is, of course, a generation gap between adults and these children of the digital generation. Give adults a new digital device and they immediately look for the instructions. Unfortunately, even when they read the instructions, many adults still fail to get the new gadget to work properly. If I had relied on my early manuals for computer operations, I would still be puzzled by the non-functional data in those manuals. Our kids, for the most part, are not bothered by such instructions because they don't read them. Some would say they can't read them, but I think it is more their intuitive knowledge of how digital things work. Who in this world of computers has not had a teenager look at you with pity and show you how a program works?

The gap between adults and the digital generation is a problem because, for the most part, our formal teachers are part of the adult world. Consequently, they have not as yet learned how to take the marvels of the digital world and adapt them to the day-to-day activities in the classroom. The good news is that in the next few years we will replace many of the teachers through retirement and other reasons.

The challenge is how to train the new generation of teachers so that they can make maximum use of the digital world around us. How can the tools of the digital world become as common in the learning and teaching of children as blackboard and chalk? How can schools begin to invest in technology at the same rate as business and industry? Business and industry capitalize the digital tools of the average worksite at between $2,500 and $5,000 per worker, depending upon the work. Schools at best spend $250 per student in capital investments in digital resources.

The virtual school is a reality in many places. How will we adapt these concepts to our traditional understanding of schools? The four walls of the classroom, after all, were a technological intervention several generations ago that modified society's concepts of universal education. Without the books and classrooms, we would still have apprenticeships. The ubiquity of the Internet makes the entire world a classroom. The challenge is how to organize our concepts of learning so students are given credit for nontraditional learning through the digital world.

What if a student participates in the school's marching band, attends a traditional classroom-based algebra class, takes French literature from an online program originating in Paris, takes a creative writing class that meets once a month, and has constant online writing and rewriting via the Internet? How will the school organize to recognize the student's performance and achievement? What if the student's creative writing teacher does not give the student a good grade, but the student publishes a number of stories in both digital and traditional published journals? How can teachers manage and structure the learning and teaching processes so that they are taking maximum advantage of the digital world?

By definition, the digital world means that we must develop more performance-based measurements of student achievement. Portfolios of the student's work can and must form the basis of the grading system of the future. The Defense Department's language school in California has five levels of achievement. Level one is to speak a language well enough to be a tourist and level five is proficiency comparable to a native speaker. Performance is the essence of measurement in this system.

It seems to me that we need to create performance-based educational measurement systems that clearly define the achievements of a learner. In the area of reading, we often claim that "Every child shall be able to read by grade 3." What do we mean by this goal? Can the child read the *New York Times* and/or a physics textbook? Does the child have the word-attack skills that allow him to read unfamiliar things? Can they read aloud fluently age-appropriate books? Can they silently read instructions and follow them? Can they find things on the Internet? Can they research things, analyze them, and draw conclusions? Can they not only read but write?

What do we mean when we say all children should have mastered reading? Reading and writing are lifetime skills that are founded on good commands of speech and language. They enable the user to express her own ideas and to receive ideas from others. Reading and writing encompass a wide range of basic skills of decoding and encoding the spoken language into print. But, ultimately, it means much more; it is the way a person logically organizes her perception of the world and shares that perception with others. It is the fountain of knowledge that grows as the learner grows. The master reader reads for comprehension and enjoys recreational reading and reading for content and information. In both instances, the reader is able to organize the information and express his own understanding of what he has comprehended.

Literacy in the modern world means not only sophisticated speech and language but also the ability to receive and express ideas through the printed word. However, in the modern world of telecommunications, the literate person can critically evaluate all forms of information from print, audio, film, television, and computer codes. The effective user of these resources becomes the literate person of a modern society.

Every child in the world is entrusted to those of us who have chosen to become teachers; whether it is graduate school medicine, advanced placement high school physics, or kindergarten, it is a sacred trust. The future of nations and the world is in our hands. There is no other calling as important as that of teacher. There is no greater challenge than to teach a child to read. Literacy is the door that opens the world to the learner, whether it is in print or electronic format. A single book and a solitary reader can discover the secrets of peace on Earth. A learner surfing the Internet could change the world. The voices of many over the Internet have helped bring down despot nations. In the digital age, we have more literacy resources than even the richest of scholars had available to them in years past. Online resources give us the world at our fingertips. The challenge is how to provide access to these riches for every child in the world.

No child is an island. In the heart of each child is a seed of great promise—but if we allow the child to grow in ignorance, that seed can become warped and distorted. Without the nurturing of literacy, the seed can fail to germinate and reach its potential. As the world's major power, America's best weapon of defense is to lead the world to universal literacy for all. There can be no child left behind in the race toward literacy for all. It is through the broad scope of literacy that we share our thoughts, ideas, experiences, and lives. It is a gift that every child is entitled to receive.

As we think of our own schools in the United States, we must also think of children around the world. We must think beyond our own shores. It has never been truer that no man is an island unto himself. Our future lies with all of the people of the world. The world has 130,000,000 children who will never spend one day with a teacher in a classroom. Therefore, if we are to leave no child behind, we must invent new and effective technological solutions to learning and teaching. The challenge of the twenty-first century is how to bring all of these children into the digital age. Guns, military power, and scientific and economic power are not enough to create a peaceful world. An enlightened world requires that all people become literate and that all people have educational opportunities. No nation is an island unto itself; we are all on the spaceship Earth together with its finite and limited resources.

This worldwide challenge requires that we reinvent learning and teaching. Technology is a major solution that can fill this gap. It is not the only solution and it does not eliminate the need for human resources. It does mean that the mentor/teacher will require a different kind of preparation to be effective in a digital world. It also requires that learning will take place anywhere and at any time. We must go where the learners are and provide the resources needed for them to learn. Technology allows learning to take place in the home, the field, the library, the community center, the workplace, and hundred of other places. The challenge is how to organize these resources and make them available to all learners.

> Hope for the World
> Each new life that is born
> Whether it is in luxury of poverty
> Holds out the hope of the world
> The promise of the new life
> Is that the best of human kind?
> Will grow and make the world a better place.
> Why not?
> Within each new life there is a promise of greatness
> There is the call that they will see the world

Not as it is, but ask the question
What can it be?
How can the world be a better place?
How can all children have the best?
In health care and education?
    Why not?
How can the earth be pure and free?
How can we dream of space?
How can we dream of peace?
How can we end war and violence?
Every new life holds within it the potential
To solve the world's problems.
    Why not?
Nurture the new life.
Let it breath free of the hatred around the world.
Let it grow in harmony.
Let it work to solve the problems of a troubled world.
Let it be all that it can be.
Each new life is a promise of greatness
That rekindles the hope of mankind.
    Why not?

—Frank B. Withrow

NOTES

1. Governor Janklow discussed this issue in his acceptance speech when he was awarded a leadership recognition at the U.S. Distance Learning Association meeting in 2001.

2. I was part of a U.S. Office of Education task force assigned to work on this project.

3. Senator Ted Kennedy was the driving force behind the creation of Star Schools legislation.

References

Adams, Marilyn Jager. 1990. *Beginning to Read: Thinking and Learning about Print*. Cambridge, Mass.: MIT Press.

Adams, Marilyn Jager, Barbara R. Foorman, Ingvar Lundberg, and Teri Beeler. 1997. *Phonemic Awareness in Young Children: A Classroom Curriculum*. Baltimore, Md.: Paul H. Brookes.

Allington, Richard L. 2002. *Big Brother and the National Reading Curriculum: How Ideology Trumped Evidence*. Portsmouth, N.H.: Heinemann.

———. 2001. *What Really Matters for Struggling Readers: Designing Research-Based Programs*. New York: Addison-Wesley.

Appalachia Educational Laboratory (AEL), at www.ael.org (accessed July 1, 2003).

Atkinson, R. C. 1974. *Adaptive Instructional Systems: Some Attempts to Optimize the Learning Process*, Technical Report 240 (November). Palo Alto, Calif.: Institute for Mathematical Studies in the Social Sciences, Stanford University.

Atwell, Nancie, ed. 1990. *Coming to Know: Writing to Learn in the Intermediate Grades*. Portsmouth, N.H.: Heinmann.

Austin, J. L. 1980. *How to Do Things with Words: The William James Lectures delivered at Harvard University in 1955*. 2nd ed. Edited by J.O. Urmson and Marina Sbisa. New York: Oxford University Press.

Bain, Ann, Laura Tyson Bailet, and Louisa Cook Moats. 1991. *Written Language Disorders*. Austin, Tex.: Pro-Ed.

Bereiter, Carl, and Marlene Scardamalia. 1982. *From Conversation to Composition: Advances in Educational Psychology*. Vol. 2. Edited by Robert Glaser. Hillsdale, N.J.: Lawrence Erlbaum.

———. *The Psychology of Written Composition*. 1987. Hillsdale, N.J.: Lawrence Erlbaum.

Berman, Jeffrey. 2001. *Risky Writing: Self-disclosure and Self-transformation in the Classroom*. Amherst: University of Massachusetts Press.

Block, Cathy Collins, Linda B. Gambrell, and Michael Pressley. 2002. *Im-*

proving Comprehension Instruction: Rethinking Research, Theory, and Classroom Practice. San Francisco, Calif.: Jossey-Bass.

Block, James H., ed. 1971. *Mastery Learning: Theory and Practice*. New York: Holt, Rinehart, and Winston.

———. 1974. *Schools, Society, and Mastery Learning*. New York: Holt, Rinehart, and Winston.

Block, James H., Helen E. Efthim, and Robert B. Burns. 1989. *Building Effective Mastery Learning Schools*. New York: Longman.

Block, James H., Susan Toft Everson, and Thomas R. Guskey. 1999. *Comprehensive School Reform: A Program Perspective*. Dubuque, Iowa: Kendall/Hunt.

Bloom, Benjamin S. 1984. "The 2 Sigma Problem: The Search for Methods as Effective as One-to-One Tutoring." *Educational Research* (July).

Blum-Kulka, Shoshana, and Catherine E. Snow, eds. 2002. *Talking to Adults: The Contribution of Multiparty Discourse to Language Acquisition*. Mahwah, N.J.: Lawrence Erlbaum.

Bolter, Jay David. 1991. *Writing Space—The Computer, Hypertext, and the History of Writing*. Hillsdale, N.J.: Lawrence Erlbaum.

Bork, Alfred. 1986. *Learning with Personal Computers*. New York: Harper and Row.

———. 1987. *Interaction: Lessons from Computer-Based Learning, Interactive Media: Working Methods and Practical Applications*. Edited by Diana Laurillard. Chicester, U.K.: Ellis Horwood.

———. 1987. *The Introduction of Computers in Schools: The Norwegian Experience*. Edited by Alfred Bork, Sandra Ann Crapper, and Jacques Hebenstreit. Paris: Organization for Economic Co-Operation and Development (November).

———. 1999. *Global Learning Society*, Student Pugwash.

———. 1999. "The Future of Learning." *EDUCOM Review* (July/August).

———. 2000. "Four Fictional Views of the Future of Learning." *The Internet and Higher Education* 2–3: 271–84.

———. 2001. "Adult Lifelong Learning, and the Future." *Campus-wide Information Systems Journal* (special issue).

———. 2001. "Highly Interactive Tutorial Distance Learning." *Information Communication and Society* 3, no. 4 (special issue).

———. 2001. "Tutorial Learning for the New Century." *Journal of Science and Technology* 10, no. 1.

———. 2001. "What Is Needed for Effective Learning on the Internet." *Educational Technology and Society* (special issue).

Bork, Alfred, and Netiva Caftori. 1999. "Computers and Major Ethical Problems in Our Society." *Simulation* 73.

Bork, Alfred, and Sigrun Gunnarsdottir. 2001. *Tutorial Distance Learning: Rebuilding Our Educational System.* New York: Kluwer Academic/Plenum Publishers.

Bork, Alfred, and Harold Weinstock, eds. 1986. *Designing Computer-Based Learning Material.* Berlin: Springer-Verlag.

Bork, Alfred, Bertrand Ibrahim, Alastair Milne, and Rika Yoshi. 1992. "The Irvine-Geneva Course Development System, Education and Society." *Information Processing* 2. Edited by R. Aiken. North Holland: Elsevier Science.

Burns, M. Susan, Peg Griffin, and Catherine E. Snow, eds. 1999. *Starting Out Right: A Guide to Promoting Children's Reading Success*, Committee on the Prevention of Reading Difficulties in Young Children, Commission on Behavioral and Social Sciences and Education. Washington, D.C.: National Academy Press.

Calkins, Lucy McCormick. 1986. *The Art of Teaching Writing.* Portsmouth, N.H.: Heinemann.

Campbell, J. R., D. L. Kelly, I. V. S. Mullis, M. O. Martin, and M. Stainsbury. 2001. *Framework and Specifications for PIRLS Assessment 2001.* Chestnut Hill, Mass.: Boston College.

Cazden, Courtney B., and Catherine E. Snow. 1990. "English Plus Issues in Bilingual Education." *Annals of the Academy of Political and Social Science.*

Chall, Jeanne Sternlicht, and Allan F. Mirsk. 1983. *Stages of Reading Development.* New York: McGraw-Hill.

Chall, Jeanne Sternlicht. 1975. "Reading and Development." Keynote address, twentieth annual convention of the International Reading Association, New York.

———. 1983. *Learning to Read: The Great Debate.* New York: McGraw-Hill.

———. 2000. *The Academic Achievement Challenge: What Really Works in the Classroom?* New York: Guilford Press.

Chall, Jeanne Sternlicht, Vicki A. Jacobs, and Luke E. Baldwin. 1990. *The Reading Crisis: Why Poor Children Fall Behind.* Cambridge, Mass.: Harvard University Press.

Cialdini, Robert B. 1993. *Influence: The Psychology of Persuasion.* New York: Morrow.

Ciarrochi, Joseph, and Joseph P. Forgas, eds. 2001. *Emotional Intelligence in Everyday Life: A Scientific Inquiry.* Philadelphia, Pa.: Psychology Press.

Clark, Margaret Macdonald. 1976. *Young Fluent Readers: What Can They Teach Us?* London: Heinemann Educational.

Clarke, John. 1990. *Patterns of Thinking*. Boston, Mass.: Allyn and Bacon.

Collins, Allan, and Dedre Getner. 1980. *A Framework for a Cognitive Theory of Writing: Cognitive Processes in Writing*. Hillsdale, N.J.: Lawrence Erlbaum.

Constanzo, William. 1989. *The Electronic Text: Learning to Write, Read, and Reason with Computers*. Englewood Cliffs, N.J.: Educational Technology Publications.

Crystal, David. 1997. *English as a Global Language*. Cambridge: Cambridge University Press.

Cummings, Jim. 2000. *Language, Power, and Pedagogy: Bilingual Children in the Crossfire*. Cleveden, U.K.: Multilingual Matters.

Curtis, Mary E., and Ann Marie Longo. 1999. *When Adolescents Can't Read: Methods and Materials that Work*. Cambridge, Mass.: Brookline Books.

Edutopia Online. 2003. *George Lucas Educational Foundation*, at http://GLEF.org (accessed July 1, 2003).

Edwards, Sharon, and Robert Maloy. 1992. *Kids Have All the Write Stuff*. London: Penguin Books.

Elbow, Peter. 1981. *Writing with Power: Techniques for Mastering the Writing Process*. New York: Oxford University Press.

Emig, Janet. 1983. *The Web of Meaning: Essays on Writing, Teaching, Learning, and Thinking*. Edited by D. Goswami and M. Butler. Montclair, N.J.: Boynton/Cook.

Esteva, Gustavo, and Madhu Suri Prakash. 1998. *Grassroots Post-Modernism: Remaking the Soil of Cultures*. London: Zed Books.

Fillmore, Lily Wong, and Catherine E. Snow. 2000. *What Teachers Need to Know about Language*. Washington, D.C.: U.S. Dept. of Education, Office of Educational Research and Improvement.

Flemming, Laraine E. 1999. *Reading for Results*. 7th ed. Boston, Mass.: Houghton Mifflin.

Flesch, Rudolf Franz. 1974. *The Art of Readable Writing*. New York: Harper and Row.

Flood, James, Shirley Brice Heath, and Diane Lapp, eds. 1997. *Handbook of Research on Teaching Literacy through the Communicative and Visual Arts*. New York: Macmillan.

Fox, Mem. 2001. *Reading Magic: Why Reading Aloud to Our Children Will Change Their Lives*. San Diego, Calif.: Harcourt.

Frank, Marcella. 1990. *Writing as Thinking: A Guided Process Approach*. Englewood Cliffs, N.J.: Prentice Hall.

Freire, Paulo. 1998. *Teachers as Cultural Workers: Letters to Those Who Dare Teach.* Boulder, Colo.: Westview Press.

Garan, Elaine M. 2002. *Resisting Reading Mandates: How to Triumph with the Truth.* Portsmouth, N.H.: Heinemann.

Gardner, Howard. 1999. *The Disciplined Mind: What All Students Should Understand.* New York: Simon and Schuster.

Gnutzmann, Claus, ed. 1997. *Teaching and Learning English as a Global Language: Native and Non-Native Perspectives.* Tubingen Stauffenberg Verlag.

Goldman-Segall, Ricki. 1998. *Points of Viewing Children's Thinking: A Digital Ethnographer's Journey.* Mahwah, N.J.: Lawrence Erlbaum.

Goleman, Daniel. 1995. *Emotional Intelligence.* New York: Bantam Books.

Goody, Jack. 1987. *The Interface between the Written and the Oral.* Cambridge: Cambridge University Press.

Hacsi, Timothy A. 2002. *Children as Pawns: The Politics of Educational Reform.* Cambridge, Mass.: Harvard University Press.

Hall, Susan L., and Louisa C. Moats. 1999. *Straight Talk about Reading.* Chicago, Ill.: Contemporary Books.

Handa, Carolyn, ed. 1990. *Computers and Community: Teaching Composition in the Twenty-First Century.* Portsmouth, N.H.: Heinmann.

Harris, Theodore L., and Richard E. Hodges, eds. 1995. *The Literacy Dictionary: The Vocabulary of Reading and Writing.* Newark, Del.: International Reading.

Hart, Betty, and Todd R. Risley. 1999. *The Social World of Children: Learning to Talk.* Baltimore, Md.: Paul H. Brookes.

———. 2000. *Meaningful Differences in the Everyday Experiences of Young Children.* Baltimore, Md.: Paul H. Brookes.

Harwayne, Shelley. 2000. *Lifetime Guarantees: Toward Ambitious Literacy Teaching.* Portsmouth, N.H.: Heinemann.

———. 2001. *Writing through Childhood: Rethinking Process and Product.* Portsmouth, N.H.: Heinemann.

Hogan, Katherine, and Michael Pressley, eds. 1997. *Scaffolding Student Learning.* Cambridge, Mass.: Brookline Books.

Holt, John Caldwell. 1995. *How Children Learn,* rev. ed. Reading, Mass.: Addison-Wesley.

Investing in Our Future: A National Research Initiative for America's Children for the 21st Century. 1997. Washington, D.C.: Executive Office of the President, Office of Science and Technology Policy.

Irvine, Margaret. 1999. *Early Childhood: A Training Manual.* Paris: UNESCO.

Kamil, Michael L., et al., eds. 2002. *Methods of Literacy. The Methodology Chapters from the Handbook of Reading Research.* Vol. 3. Mahwah, N.J.: Lawrence Erlbaum.

Kamil, Michael L., Judith A. Langer, and Timothy Shanahan. 1985. *Understanding Reading and Writing Research.* Boston, Mass.: Allyn and Bacon.

Kavanagh, James F., and Ignatius G. Mattingly, eds. 1972. *Language by Ear and by Eye: The Relationships between Speech and Reading.* Cambridge, Mass.: MIT Press.

Kimbell-Lopez, Kimberly. 1999. *Connecting with Traditional Literature: Using Folktales, Fables, and Legends to Strengthen Student's Reading and Writing.* Boston, Mass.: Allyn and Bacon.

Kline, Peter. 2002. *Why America's Children Can't Think.* Makawao, Hawaii: Inner Ocean Publishing.

Kurzweil, Ray. 1999. *The Age of Spiritual Machines.* New York: Viking.

Labaree, David F. 1997. *How to Succeed in School without Really Learning: The Credentials Race in American Schools.* New Haven, Conn.: Yale University Press.

Langer, Judith. 1986. *Children Reading and Writing: Structures and Strategies.* Norwood, N.J.: Ablex.

Lederer, Richard. 1989. *Crazy English.* New York: Pocket Books.

Lessig, Lawrence. 2001. *The Future of Ideas: The Fate of the Commons in a Connected World.* New York: Random House.

Literacy Center. *Early Childhood Education Network,* at www.familiartales.com (accessed July 1, 2003).

Lucas, Joni. 1993. *Teaching Writing: Emphasis Swings to Process, Writing as Tool for Learning.* Alexandria, Va.: Association for Supervision and Curriculum Development.

Lund, Carsten. 1992. *The Power of Interaction.* Cambridge, Mass.: MIT Press.

Madden, Nancy, Robert Stevens, and Robert Slavin. 1986. *A Comprehensive Cooperative Learning Approach to Elementary Reading and Writing: Effects on Student Achievement.* Washington, D.C.: Center for Research on Elementary and Middle Schools, Office of Educational Research and Improvement.

Maeroff, Gene. 2003. *A Classroom of One: How Online Learning Is Changing Schools and Colleges.* New York: Palgrave Macmillan.

Mahony, Diana, and Virginia Mann. 1998. "Children's Linguistic Humor and Reading Research: A Match Made in Heaven." *Current Psychology of Cognition* 17, no. 2: 287–311.

Mann, Virginia. 1993. "Phonemic Awareness and Future Reading Ability." *Journal of Learning Disabilities* 26: 259–69.

———. 1998. "Language Problems: A Key to Early Reading Problems." In *Learning about Learning Disabilities*, edited by B. Wong. 2nd ed. San Diego: Academic Press.

McGinnis, Mildred A. 1963. *Aphasic Children: Identification and Training by the Association Method.* Washington, D.C.: Alexander Graham Bell Association for the Deaf.

Meredith, Geoffrey. 1999. "The Demise of Writing." *The Futurist* 33 (October).

Meyer, Anne, and David H. Rose. 1998. *Learning to Read in the Computer Age.* Cambridge, Mass.: Brookline Books.

Mid-continent Research for Education and Learning, at www.mcrel.org (accessed July 1, 2003).

Miller, Ron. 2002. *Free Schools, Free People, and Democracy after the 1960s.* Albany: State University of New York Press.

Moats, Louisa Cook. 2000. *Speech to Print: Language Essentials for Teachers.* Baltimore, Md.: Paul H. Brookes.

National Reading Panel. 2000. *Report of the National Reading Panel: Reports of the Subgroups.* Washington, D.C.: National Institute of Child Health and Human Development, National Institutes of Health.

———. 2000. *Teaching Children to Read: An Evidence-Based Assessment of the Scientific Research Literature on Reading and Its Implications for Reading Instruction.* Washington, D.C.: National Institute of Child Health and Human Development, National Institutes of Health.

National Telecommunications and Information Administration. 1999. *Falling through the Net: Defining the Digital Divide: A Report on the Telecommunications and Information Technology Gap in America.* Washington, D.C.: U.S. Department of Commerce.

———. 1998. *Falling through the Net II: New Data on the Digital Divide.* Washington, D.C.: U.S. Dept. of Commerce. 1998.

———. 1999. *Falling through the Net III: Defining the Digital Divide.* Washington, D.C.: U.S. Dept. of Commerce, 1999.

Negroponte, Nicholas. 1995. *Being Digital.* New York: Knopf.

Norman, Donald A., and Stephen W. Draper, eds. 1986. *User Centered System Design: New Perspectives on Human-Computer Interaction.* Hillsdale, N.J.: Lawrence Erlbaum.

Oakes, Jeannie, et al. 2000. *Becoming Good American Schools: The Struggle for Civic Virtue in Reform.* San Francisco, Calif.: Jossey-Bass.

Oakes, Jeannie, and Martin Lipton. 1999. *Teaching to Change the World*. Boston, Mass.: McGraw-Hill.

Ogle, Lawrence, and Anindita Sen. 2003. *International Comparisons in Fourth-Grade Reading Literacy: Findings from the Progress in International Literacy Study of 2001*. Washington, D.C.: U.S. Department of Education.

Pellegrino, James W., Naomi Chudowsky, and Robert Glaser, eds. 2001. *Knowing What Students Know: The Science and Design of Educational Assessment*. Washington, D.C.: National Academy Press.

Prakash, Madhu Suri, and Gustavo Esteva. 1998. *Escaping: Living as Learning within Grassroots Cultures*. New York: Peter Lang.

Putnam, Lillian R., ed. 1987. *Readings on Language and Literacy: Essays in Honor of Jean Chall*. Cambridge, Mass.: Brookline Books.

Rafoth, Bennett, and Donald Rubin, eds. 1988. *The Social Construction of Written Communication*. Norwood, N.J.: Ablex.

Rayner, Keith, Barbara R. Foorman, Charles A. Perfetti, David Pesetsky, and Mark S. Seidenberg. 2001. "How Psychological Science Informs the Teaching of Reading." *Psychological Science in the Public Interest* 2 (November).

Reeves, Byron, and Clifford Nass. 1996. *The Media Equation: How People Treat Computers, Television, and New Media Like Real People and Places*. Cambridge: Cambridge University Press.

Reiser, Robert A., and John V. Dempsey, eds. 2002. *Trends and Issues in Instructional Design and Technology*. Upper Saddle River, N.J.: Merrill/ Prentice Hall.

Reising, Christopher. *Song Design*, at www.songdesign.com (accessed July 1, 2003).

Richek, Margaret Ann, JoAnne Schudt Caldwell, Joyce Holt Jennings, and Janet W. Lerner. 2002. *Reading Problems: Assessment and Teaching Strategies*. Boston, Mass.: Allyn and Bacon.

Rosen, Connie and Harold Rosen. 1973. *The Language of Primary School Children*. Harmondsworth, U.K.: Penguin for the Schools Council.

Rossman, Parker. 1992. *The Emerging Worldwide Electronic University: Information Age Global Higher Education*. Westport, Conn.: Greenwood Press.

Schank, Roger. 1990. *Tell Me a Story*. New York: Charles Scribner's Sons.

Schwartz, H. J. 1983. "Teaching Organization with Word Processing." *Computers, Reading, and Language Arts* 1, no. 3 (winter).

Shonkoff, Jack P., and Deborah A Phillips, eds. 2000. *From Neurons to Neighborhoods: The Science of Early Childhood Development*. Washington, D.C.: National Academy Press.

Shore, Rima. 1997. *Rethinking the Brain: New Insights into Early Development*. New York: Families and Work Institute.

———. 1998. *Ready Schools*. Washington, D.C.: The National Goals Panel.

Slavin, Robert. 1990. *Cooperative Learning; Theory, Research and Practice*. Englewood Cliffs, N.J.: Prentice Hall.

Snow, Catherine E. 2001. *Reading for Understanding: Toward a Research and Development Program in Reading Comprehension*. Santa Monica, Calif.: Rand.

Snow, Catherine E., et al. 1991. *Unfulfilled Expectations: Home and School Influences on Literacy*. Cambridge, Mass.: Harvard University Press.

Snow, Catherine, Susan Burns, and Peg Griffin. 1998. *Preventing Reading Difficulties in Young Children*. Washington, D.C.: National Academy Press.

———. 1999. *Language and Literacy Environments in Preschools*. Champaign: University of Illinois.

Snow, Catherine E., and Charles A. Ferguson. 1997. "Talking to Children: Language Input and Acquisition." Papers from a conference sponsored by the Committee on Sociolinguistics of the Social Science Research Council, Cambridge University Press.

Sokolov, Jeffrey L., and Catherine E. Snow, eds. 1994. *Handbook of Research in Language Development Using CHILDES*. Hillsdale, N.J.: Lawrence Erlbaum.

Solomon, G. 1985. "Writing with Computers." *Electronic Learning* 5, no. 3 (November–December).

Spender, Dale. 1995. *Nattering on the Net: Women, Power, and Cyberspace*. North Melbourne, Vic.: Spinifex Press.

Spring, Joel H. 2000. *The Universal Right to Education: Justification, Definition, and Guidelines*. Mahwah, N.J.: Lawrence Erlbaum.

Stanovich, Keith E. 2000. *Progress in Understanding Reading: Scientific Foundations and New Frontiers*. New York: Guilford Press.

Star Schools Program Sites. 2003. *U.S. Department of Education* (June 13) at www.ed.gov/EdRes/EdFed/Star.html (accessed July 1, 2003).

Stephenson, Neal. 1995. *The Diamond Age, or A Young Lady's Illustrated Primer*. New York: Bantam.

Steward, Elizabeth Petrick. 1995. *Beginning Writers in the Zone of Proximal Development*. Hillsdale, N.J.: Lawrence Erlbaum.

Sweet, Anne P., and John T. Guthrie. 1996. "How Children's Motivations Relate to Literacy Development and Instruction." *The Reading Teacher* 49 (May): 660.

Sweet, Anne Poselli, and Catherine E. Snow. 2003. *Rethinking Reading Comprehension*. New York: Guilford Press

Tuman, Myron, ed. 1992. *Literacy Online*. Pittsburgh, Pa.: University of Pittsburgh Press.

Verhoeven, Ludo, and Catherine E. Snow, eds. 2001. *Literacy and Motivation: Reading Engagement in Individuals and Groups*. Mahwah, N.J.: Lawrence Erlbaum.

Vygotsky, Lev. 1962. *Thought and Language*. Cambridge, Mass.: M.I.T. Press.

———. 1978. *Mind in Society*. Cambridge, Mass.: Harvard University Press.

Waterman, John A., and Mike Talbot. 1987. *Speech and Language-based Interaction with Computers*. Chichester, U.K.: Ellis Horwood.

Wertsch, James V., ed. 1985. *Culture, Communication and Cognition: Vygotskian Perspectives*. Cambridge: Cambridge University Press.

Whiteman, Marcia Farr. 1981. *Reading and Writing: Vol. 1, Variation in Reading and Writing*. Hillsdale, N.J.: Lawrence Erlbaum.

Williams, Rosalind H. 1990. *Notes on the Underground: An Essay on Technology, Society, and the Imagination*. Cambridge, Mass.: MIT Press.

———. 2002. *Retooling: A Historian Confronts Technological Change*. Cambridge, Mass.: MIT Press.

Withrow, Frank B. 1967. *The Use of Instructional Media with the Special Hearing-Impaired Child*. Jacksonville: Illinois School for the Deaf.

———. 1981. *Learning Technology and the Hearing Impaired*. Washington, D.C.: Alexander Graham Bell Association for the Deaf.

———. 2003. *Phonic Picks* at www.phonicpicks.com (accessed July 1, 2003).

Withrow, Frank B., Harvey Long, and Gary Marx. 1999. *Preparing Schools and School Systems for the Twenty-first Century*. Arlington, Va.: American Association of School Administrators.

Withrow, Frank B., and Carolyn J. Nygren. 1976. *Language, Materials, and Curriculum Development for the Handicapped Learner*. Columbus, Ohio: Charles E. Merrill.

Wolfe, Patricia. 2001. *Brain Matters: Translating Research into Classroom Practice*. Alexandria, Va.: Association for School Curriculum Development.

Zucker, Andrew, Robert Kozma, et al. 2003. *The Virtual High School: Teaching Generation V*. New York: Teachers College Press.

INDEX

About the Author

Dr. Frank B. Withrow has been a classroom teacher, elementary supervisor, researcher, and an educational administrator. As the director of Research and Clinical Services in the Department of Children and Family Services in the state of Illinois, he developed a parent-pupil program for deaf infants and their parents. His research includes electrophysiological testing of hearing in infants, paired associate learning, immediate visual memory spans, and the uses of programmed 3-D computer-generated lessons.

Dr. Withrow was the director of Educational Programs for the NASA Classroom of the Future from 1996 to 1998. He served in the U.S. Department of Education from 1966 to 1992 as the senior learning technologist. He administered technology programs for the disabled, including Captioned Films for the Deaf where he developed captioning techniques for television. In addition, he funded the development of reading machines for blind people. He was the executive director of the National Advisory Committee for the Handicapped in 1975 at the time PL 94-142 was passed. He served as the secretary's liaison for the National Technical Institute for the Deaf, Rochester Institute for Technology, Gallaudet University, and the Model Secondary School for the Deaf.

As a Senior Battelle Memorial Fellow, he studied the influence of electronic media on child growth and development. He developed a demonstration of interactive cable television programs and edited a book on the influence of television on child growth and development.

He was the program manger for the department's television series, including *Sesame Street*, *Footsteps* (a series on child growth and development for parents) and *The Voyages of the Mimi* (a multiple-media elementary science and mathematics series). He also directed bilingual television programming that included Hispanic, French, Native American, Asian, and African American themes. All programs included captions.

He was the director of technology for the Young Astronaut Council where he developed an online series of lessons for students and teachers.

He developed and managed the Star Schools distance-learning program for the U.S. Department of Education. He represented the United States of America as a learning technologist at a number of world conferences, including OECD, UNESCO, and the Council of Europe.

Dr. Withrow has worked as an adjunct professor at Washington University, St. Louis, Missouri, MacMurray College, Jacksonville, Illinois, and Ohio State University, Columbus, Ohio.

He has received many honors and awards, including the United States Distance Learning Association's Leadership award. He is a member of USDLA's Hall of Fame. He has edited several books and written more than 300 professional articles. He has made numerous presentations and speeches, including keynote addresses at professional conferences. He has more than 200 video and film credits.

He was on the board of the Northern Panhandle Head Start Program, Wheeling, West Virginia. He was a member of the national board for the National Technical Institute for the Deaf (NTID) at the Rochester Institute for Technology. He was a board member of the Consortium on School Networking (CoSN). The CoSN annual educator award is named the Frank Withrow Award for Excellence.

He was the program manager for two one-hour television specials on the "World of Work," which were designed to help youth and other people seeking employment understand the modern clusters of jobs and the training required to obtain such jobs. He was an advisory to the District of Columbia Public Schools multimedia project on developing employability skills for youth. He serves as an advisor to a District of Columbia school board member.

He received his B.S. in education of the deaf, M.S. in speech and hearing, and a Ph.D. in audiology from Washington University in St. Louis. He holds advanced clinical certification in both speech and hearing from the American Speech and Hearing Association.

The reader can reach Dr. Withrow at:

Able Learning Company
A Better Learning Experience Company
232 E Street, NE
Washington, DC 20002-4923
(202) 547-8078
FAX (202) 546-6059
FBWithrow@PhonicPicks.com